STRESS AND NERVOUS DISORDERS

Jan de Vries was born in Holland in 1937 and grew up in occupied territory during the difficult war years. Graduating in pharmacy, he turned to alternative medicine. His most influential teacher was Dr Alfred Vogel in Switzerland, and they have worked together closely for 35 years.

In 1970 he and his family moved to Scotland and settled in Troon where he set up a residential clinic. He also has clinics in Newcastle, Edinburgh and London. He lectures throughout the world and is a regular broadcaster on BBC radio. His books have sold over a quarter of a million copies to date.

Books available from the same author

By Appointment Only series
Arthritis, Rheumatism and Psoriasis
Asthma and Bronchitis
Cancer and Leukaemia
Heart and Blood Circulatory Problems
Migraine and Epilepsy
The Miracle of Life
Multiple Sclerosis
Neck and Back Problems
Realistic Weight Control
Skin Diseases
Stomach and Bowel Disorders
Stress and Nervous Disorders
Traditional Home and Herbal Remedies
Viruses, Allergies and the Immune System

Nature's Gift series
Air – The Breath of Life
Body Energy
Food
Water – Healer or Poison?

Well Woman series
Menopause
Menstrual and Pre-Menstrual Tension
Pregnancy and Childbirth

The Jan de Vries Healthcare series
How to Live a Healthy Life – A Handbook to Better Health
Questions and Answers on Family Health
The Five Senses

Also available from the same author
Life Without Arthritis – The Maori Way
Who's Next?

STRESS AND NERVOUS DISORDERS

JAN DE VRIES

MAINSTREAM
PUBLISHING

EDINBURGH AND LONDON

This edition 1992

First published in Great Britain in 1985 by
MAINSTREAM PUBLISHING COMPANY (EDINBURGH) LTD
7 Albany Street
Edinburgh EH1 3UG
Reprinted 1989, 1994, 1997 and 2001

ISBN 1 85158 651 2

A catalogue record for this book is available from the British Library

Typeset in 10/11pt Andover by Studioscope
Printed and bound in Great Britain by
Creative Print and Design Wales, Ebbw Vale

Contents

Foreword

TWENTY-FIVE years ago in Holland, when I started practising alternative medicine, I was regarded as a pioneer of this type of healing and the Dutch people soon accepted my unconventional methods.

It was not long, however, until my thirst for knowledge became so great that I felt compelled to widen my horizons and travel to satisfy this need.

I travelled the globe acquiring knowledge and studying in every corner until, fifteen years ago, I settled in Scotland. Once more I found myself to be a pioneer; this time I had to convince the Scots that there were other, safer, treatments for their ailments.

Like the Dutch, the Scottish people were receptive to me and my methods and I feel there was a natural rapport between us from the start.

It seems only natural too, that I am writing this book because after almost all of the 400 plus lectures which I have given in Scotland, I was asked why I had not written a book about my work.

I practise many different forms of alternative medicine and it would be impossible to contain the areas of my work in just one book.

So after some careful deliberation, bearing in mind the reasons why people consult me, I decided that problems concerning nerves were a worthy subject for my first book.

BY APPOINTMENT ONLY

The past fifteen years have been very busy indeed for me and I have built up a mammoth collection of over 125,000 case histories. During preparation for this book, therefore, I took the opportunity to re-live the problems of my patients by looking back at my records. Consequently, throughout the fifteen chapters you will encounter many stories relating to these problems. Perhaps they will help to explain my methods of working.

In any case, I hope you will find the many anecdotes interesting and possibly of some value. I hope also, that by reading about those who have won the war against nerve problems and all the other related disorders, those who are suffering right now will find fresh hope.

Jan de Vries

Introduction

by

Dr Hans Moolenburgh MD
Holland

I am grateful to my friend, Jan de Vries, for asking me to write this introduction. It is extremely important that bridges should be built between what is nowadays called orthodox medicine and what people call alternative medicine. Neither term is accurate. Orthodox medicine is a result of the technical revolution and has not been with us for long. Alternative medicine has been with us as long as we can remember and could be better defined as original medicine.

Orthodox medicine is taught at our universities and it has brought many blessings, but also great dangers. The doctor in Germany who put a notice on his door — "Danger! Here lives a doctor!" was overdoing it a bit and his colleagues were not amused, but he had a point. Let me give you an example.

I have been a general practitioner for 32 years. One of my patients was a very sweet, soft spoken school teacher. She was certainly no candidate for a beauty contest, having a large chin and even larger nose. One day (she had been in my practice for about 20 years) she came to me complaining of bloody stools. Straight away I sent her to a specialist who took an X-ray, looked into her intestines, and found a bleeding polyp. The surgeon took the thing out and happily there was no evidence of cancer.

So far so good. But then a sort of "little Red Ridinghood" situation developed, with the specialist saying: "But lady, what a big chin you have got, and what a big nose you have got." What a pity he did not say — "And what a big mouth you have got" . . . for then she could have eaten him!

She was sent to an academic centre (without my knowledge) where another specialist took some blood tests and announced that she had to have another operation, this time to remove her hypophysis.

That same day she came to my office in tears. When she explained the situation I nearly exploded with rage. I told her that there was no question of operations which would leave her a hormonal wreck and in need of a lot of hormone tablets for the rest of her life. She had always looked like that and I told her I would not allow this. I will spare you the emotional pressure she was put under by both regional and academic specialists, but she refused to allow them to operate on her.

Some time ago, six years after these events, I saw her racing on her bike along one of our canals. I yelled at her to stop which she did. I asked her how she was and she said: "Just fine, doctor."

I presume that the specialist in Leyden was in need of a series of operations on the hypophysis. They call that being in need of "human material".

And in this little story you can see both the blessing and the curse of modern medicine. It was a blessing that with modern techniques the polyp could be found; that with modern surgery it could be taken out; and that with modern analysis it could be pronounced non-malignant. But it is a curse that we cannot stop any more. We go on and on where even angels dare not tread and undo the good work we started. We have become superintellectuals, but we have lost our wisdom. Our heads are in the clouds but we have lost contact with our feet.

And that is where books like this fill the gap. Of course, Jan de Vries is a sophisticated alternative therapist, but what he gives in this book about nervous disorders is more than alternative therapy. He combines alternative treatment with grass-root level wisdom — the thing we lost when we began insuring our bodies and thinking that someone else is responsible for their well-being. Jan does not hesitate to quote some wisdom from his grandmother. It is not widely realised that we were a healthier people when illness was still treated by the ancient remedies of our grandmothers and elderly aunts and that only in difficult cases the doctor was called.

Perhaps the reason we are so bad at treating nervous disorders is that we have lost contact with the grass-root level. You can never treat a patient with a nervous disorder successfully as long as his feet are not on the ground.

After Jan has taken us through the alternative circuit we see that this original medicine has also gone through an important development. It has learned from the exact analytical method without betraying its ancient roots. It has kept contact with the man in the street and yet is rubbing shoulders with the best brains all over the world. Never during an alternative treatment will one hear a patient complain: "I was just a number there". And how much this complaint is heard in modern hospitals!

A London businessman of Scottish descent was suddenly attacked by a horrible delusion. He could not sleep because he thought there was a man-eating tiger under his bed. So he went to his G.P. who sent him to a psychiatrist. He was given psycho-analysis and for one-and-a-half-years, three times a week, the man talked about everything that came into his head. They discovered some interesting things from his youth which could have explained the tiger delusion. But the animal was still there, making sleep impossible.

Then one day the businessman went to visit his mother in Aberdeen. When he arrived home he rang his psychiatrist to say that he did not need him any more because he was cured. The psychiatrist was astonished and asked how this could be.

The businessman replied: "I met my old minister and he said, 'Kenneth, you do not look your usual bright self.' I told him about the tiger under my bed and he said, 'Well laddie, that is easy. Put your mattress on to the floor, then there will be no room for the tiger.'"

What I really mean is this: Orthodox medicine is male, often harsh, and very intellectual. Alternative medicine is gentle, female and very intuitive. It is high time they married, then more patients would benefit. I believe that this book will help prepare for the marriage. I hope it will be widely read and will be a blessing for many.

1

Nerve Problems

WE ARE ALL followers of fashion. Like it or not, the latest
trends, whether in clothes, eating habits, or medicine, influence
us all to a certain extent. Take a visit to the doctor, for instance.
Who would dare to question the prescribed treatment? Indeed,
most people leave the surgery without the faintest idea whether
the tiny white tablet they will be swallowing faithfully for a
specified period is a hardy annual or the result of the latest
scientific breakthrough. The chances are that in taking the drug
you are following a fashion.

Let's look back at fashion in medicine. Medicinal fashions, like
styles of clothing, revolve through the years. For example,
"Valerian", a herbal root with a peculiar ability to treat hysterical
conditions, was what Hippocrates, the father of medicine,
advised his peer, Plato, the Greek scientist, to give to women
who were nervous, impatient and moody because they could not
bear children. Today "Valerian" is making a comeback and is a
principal ingredient of many herbal sedatives. Furthermore,
recent research has shown that Valerian has "anti-cancer"
properties.

In the middle ages Egyptian mummies were in great demand
because it was thought that life could be lengthened by
consuming powdered mummy residues. There is no sign of this
particular fashion being recycled though! Laxatives, burning
irons, bloodletting and enemas were next to share the limelight.
King Louis VIII of France had, believe it or not, 212 enemas and

47 bloodlettings each year. Louis XIV also held the enema in the highest respect and his people were advised to have at least one per day.

During Queen Victoria's reign, her subjects were obsessed with the problem of lazy bowels. The English surgeon, Arbuthnot Lane, tried to solve this problem once and for all with an operation he performed more than a thousand times i.e. the removal of the large intestine. He was certainly successful in curing constipation but what was he then to do about more than a thousand cases of acute diarrhoea?

In the twenties fashions changed again and this time the poor tonsils were on the chopping block. On every possible occasion they were whipped out and in 1930 more than half of British children had lost their tonsils. The health of very few children improved as a result because only a tiny minority ever really needed the operation.

There is, however, one trend in medicine which has been with us for a good many years and which, unfortunately, shows no immediate sign of being phased out — the consumption of tranquillisers and sleeping tablets. If these so-called remedies were of long-term help to patients, we would have a lot less depressions, suicides, nervous breakdowns and hysterias. Instead, our brains are steadily being ruined with excessive pill swallowing which is very often not even controlled by physicians. There is no evidence to show that such drugs can make us happier, healthier or calmer. This particular trend for drugs which are used in an effort to calm anxiety is still rampant, but I believe that fashion in medicine generally is on a turning point. The younger generation especially are beginning to ask for remedies which are free from the risk of side-effects or long-term dangers.

Not long ago I attended an important medical conference in Los Angeles, USA, where I met a doctor who was successfully treating people with nerve complaints, including depression, obsessions, anxieties, sleeplessness, and stress, with a simple injection. These injections had been welcomed with open arms and elevated the doctor to a position of fame and fortune, enabling him to establish one of the largest clinics in America. I was completely intrigued, and after much persuasion he told me what the magic ingredients of the injection were: it was to do with something with which I was all too familiar — the herb "Valerian". My thoughts turned to Hippocrates and his advice to Plato, proving my point that fashions in medicine are always revolving.

Nevertheless, while alternative medicine is growing in popularity, the majority of people in this country, whether young, middle-aged, or old, are still swallowing pills like sweets. For most people, a week rarely passes without a visit to the family medicine cabinet or the chemist in search of a tablet or powder to relieve a headache or other ailment. Many can't even enjoy a good night's sleep without the aid of a tablet. In fact, there are at least one-and-a-half-million prescriptions for sleeping tablets issued each year in Scotland alone.

It is not common sense to take drugs so readily. Our bodies are our responsibility and we must exercise understanding over how we look after them. It is sensible to seek out more natural ways of healing and there are many natural methods which can help to reduce a person's intake of tablets and reliance on drugs. Great caution must be shown when endeavouring to cut down, or stop completely, drugs which have been taken regularly. It does not take long for the body to grow accustomed to drugs and it can be dangerous to interfere irresponsibly with a dependence on any particular substance. The golden rule is to always seek expert advice before deciding on any course of action.

I am also filled with alarm when I hear of the fashionable stimulants and narcotics which are drawing the younger generation towards serious drug addiction. There is no happiness to be found with these evil substances and they can lead all too easily to mental and physical illnesses and even to death.

Another section of the community who are not coping well with the modern world are the children. They are brought to see me, tired and miserable, and often suffering from stress. It dismays me to see young ones like this, and to hear that they cannot manage their school-work. The problem in such cases usually lies, not with the child, but with the mother who is lacking in some basic education regarding the upbringing of children. The ability to be a good mother doesn't require academic knowledge but simply an awareness of the basic principles of good health. Young people have, of course, been suffering from stress and tension for many years. Long before I came to Britain I was involved, along with Dr R A Benthem Oosterhuis from Amsterdam, in the setting up of a committee within our homoeopathic society to help young people with such problems. When he was approaching the grand age of 100 and represented the perfect example of a healthy mind and body truly in harmony, I remember well him saying to me: "Please, Jan, in your lectures tell young mothers that children need good food and enough rest." He was so right. We need look no further than the eating habits of the average child and the late nights spent watching television to see why tiredness and tension are prevalent.

The nervous system of young and old alike works similarly to the battery of a car. It needs to be charged. But how? Sufficient rest and a complete diet are fundamental.

Many times, during periods I have spent in Switzerland, I have watched the farmers gathering flowering oats at the end of the harvest. The Swiss farmers conserve these oats in some brandy or alcohol and the end product is one of the most marvellous natural tranquillisers known to man. Yet another excellent natural remedy is Avena Sativa which is also derived from oats. Britain, and especially Scotland, is famed for its oats which through generations were the mainstay of the traditional diet. There is no better start to the day than a bowl of porridge but sadly this habit is fading fast and modern breakfast foods, often sugar-coated, are taking over.

Modern foods are rapidly waging a war against health and daily the nervous systems of our young people are put under attack as they consume plates of chips dripping with grease and tumblers of fizzy cola drinks. How in the world can we feed our nervous systems like this? How can we charge a battery with absolutely nothing?

I would like to mention here an experience which I had while I was in Edinburgh to lecture to students. One lunchtime, in search of some fresh air, I took a walk along the most majestic highway in Scotland — Princes Street — where I overheard, by chance, three different conversations. Fortunately, or perhaps unfortunately, I am Dutch and as a people we are not known for our impeccable manners. Perhaps I should not have eavesdropped that day but I must admit I am glad I did.

The first conversation I caught was between two middle-aged ladies who had been out for lunch together. One said to the other: "I feel absolutely sick. That was a dreadful lunch we had in that restaurant." The friend replied: "Why then did you eat it?" She was promptly told: "I had to eat it because I had paid for it."

I next encountered two younger ladies who were bitterly complaining about a television programme screened the previous night. One was explaining to her companion that because the programme had been so awful, she had been forced to take a few sleeping tablets in order to get to sleep. "Why did you look at it?" asked the companion. She was told: "But I wanted to see the end."

My final encounter concerned me more than I can express in words. I overheard two lovely young students talking as they walked along. I was shocked when the dark-haired girl told her blonde friend that she thought life was no longer worth living. She said that she wished she could end it all. I further learned that she was on drugs from her doctor, suffered depression day after day, and felt as if she had nothing to live for. I couldn't resist talking to her and, after excusing myself for being so forthright, I said I was terribly sorry to hear that such a charming girl had no desire to live. Luckily the girl was not offended at the interruption and seemed prepared to listen. As I told her that I was happy for every day of life and thanked God each morning when I opened my curtains to the outside world, I saw her becoming interested. We went on to have a long conversation during which I offered her as much advice as possible. Later I sent her the remedies which could help her. Eventually, as a result of this treatment her *joie de vivre* returned and she was able to give up the pills and potions which were helping to destroy her life. Now she is just as anxious as I am to live life to the full. This story is an example of the tragedy to which young people who have abused their nervous systems are wide open.

In the first story, the lady with the upset stomach obviously gave money priority over her body. She was ignorant of the absolute necessity to eat the correct food and, I am sad to say, is a typical example of someone who has little true commonsense. The second conversation displays clearly that it is so easy for people to become caught up in the general rut of living to the point that they forget to be sensible. Many people today have three important shortcomings. They are not sensible; they are irresponsible; and they lack commonsense.

We should all feel responsible for the life which is given to us and try to live it sensibly. Pill-popping is shirking from that duty. Our bodies need to be carefully looked after. We have trillions of body cells and every tick of the clock ten thousands of these cells die. It is not difficult to understand, therefore, why renewal of cells is of paramount importance.

My long experience of working in alternative medicine has led me to the conclusion that the answer to many health problems can be found in one word — *ENERGY*. It is common to everything which is alive — humans, animals, plants and cells, for instance. Dr Walter Schwarz, a medical doctor, chemist and physicist, wrote, among other things, in his welcoming paper to the first colloquium of the 1st International Teaching and Research Centre for Total Therapy, in 1971:

> Every Illness or health problem has a location factor and can be influenced by the environmental pollution at the time and by the manifold disturbances in the earth's magnetic and electrical fields. Furthermore, the second focal point of the research centre is concerned with man's place in the Cosmos. Man is a component of the Cosmos inseparably linked as a Creature with the Creation.

If this link is weakened or completely broken off, illness or death will inevitably occur. Man receives frequencies from the Cosmos, which means that everything which is alive needs energy. It is a great gift to man, this constant flow of energy, but we have to learn to direct it to our minds and bodies, to allow them to function together effectively. If, somewhere along the line, this energy flow is disturbed, it is not surprising that the result is an unbalanced, mixed-up person. Another name for this energy is the Life Force and it must be handled very carefully. In taking a nerve pill, tranquilliser, or sleeping tablet, we attack the tremendous field of energy which is really what the body is.

I once learned from an old monk that the ancient scriptures

said that God has given each creature in nature everything it needs to exist, the food in the fields and the herbs for healing, for example. According to these scriptures a major obstacle in this was that He had given all these gifts of nature to the "sensible" man.

Where there are nerve problems the Life Force is under great pressure and only when the problems begin to subside can a healthy balance be restored. This is very evident to the person who practises Kirlian Photography. In one case I recall the practice was carried out by two lay people who did not have much understanding of health in general. The patient was a Scotsman who lived in London and he had the most negative personality, was depressed and miserable, and was barely interested in living. This specialised form of photography was used to take a print of his hands and feet, showing the aura, or energy flow, which surrounds them. It was significant to note in this case that there was practically no evidence of any energy on the photograph. One of the two who were taking an interest in the poor man had a limited knowledge of reflexography, a natural treatment which focuses on pressure points in the hands and feet, and he attempted to use this method to help his patient. It was most interesting to look at the second photograph, taken after treatment, and see the Life Force which had been generated as a result of this reflex therapy. After further natural treatment the man was well on the road to recovery, and his new inner harmony was clearly reflected in his facial expression. Even lay people can have unexpected success.

During my study in China I learned that the people of Peking believe that the supreme temple is that of harmony. A close second is perfection, something which you would think could not be bettered. The Chinese, however, believe that perfection is not the ultimate desire. Harmony between mind and body is their clear winner. I can understand why. It is vital that there is harmony in each individual. Nevertheless, it is not always easy to achieve complete harmony and sometimes special methods have to be employed to help realise this. It is so important that the energy flow between the two main life streams, life and death, is in harmony.

In the old Chinese philosophy of acupuncture we talk about

19

yin and yang streams, just as you can talk about light and dark. In the human body we talk about the two main energy streams, life and death. Without this harmony illness can be waiting just round the corner.

"What is illness?" This question is always put to me by students. My answer agrees with the Chinese: illness is disharmony.

In the Western world disharmony is commonplace but the opposite is true of many other parts of the world. I have visited people in distant lands who live much closer to nature than we do and, on each occasion, I've discovered a great feeling of harmony in them. Ancient practices, such as meditation, often help to achieve this harmony. There is an expression in Taiwan which says that meditation brings concentration. I have personally seen the many hours which are spent in meditation there and I have admired the wonderful concentration of the people which leads to a minimal incidence of nervous disorders. In this country, where numbers of people suffering such disorders rise by the minute, we are sadly lacking the discipline and concentration which are by-products of meditation and other body and mind conditioning rituals.

A mind which has suffered has to learn to concentrate all over again and I suggest the following simple method to help patients who are back at the beginning.

Where concentration has suffered, there is rarely any desire to read, especially if the book or article is of no interest. My advice is to select such a piece of writing, something which is completely uninspiring, and read the first two sentences. Then ask yourself what you can remember of what you have just read. Keep trying, with more sentences, or even with a whole page. This is an excellent method of retraining the memory. Try it on the uninteresting parts, which there are sure to be in the book and you will be surprised at how this method draws back the powers of concentration that have been stealthily slipping away.

There is no doubt that today our brains are not in demand the way they used to be. We live in an age of computers and calculators which make life easy and require a minimum of brain power. I have reservations about the regular use of these instruments by the young and I would go so far as to say that I think they can be dangerous. The brains of our young people are not being stretched as they should. They are lacking in training of the mind, training which is so important in the search for harmony between mind and body. In Eastern countries this search goes no further than the traditional rituals, and the elderly, who have practised them for a lifetime, have minds as sharp as children. According to an old Chinese saying, meditation, which brings concentration, in turn gives us rest, peace — and hope.

I feel that it would be helpful to explain in simple terms, how the nervous system works. It consists of two parts. The first is the cerebro spinal system of nerves. This is under the control of the brain and is responsible for all voluntary movement and actions such as walking, speaking, feeling and touching. The second is the autonomic or involuntary system in the brain which acts without conscious thought and controls the working of the heart, stomach, and vital functions of the body generally.

Both systems are inter-connected and together motivate the body by means of what we call the nerve force, a kind of electric current. Although the origin of the nerve force is shrouded in mystery, it is really life itself and we know that it is vital. Most nerve diseases or disorders don't necessarily have to result in a complete breakdown of this nerve force but they are signals which should warn us that it is in great need of attention.

There is a growing awareness of the "Immune System" and of its importance when treating patients. In personal experience of working with the immune system, I have been thrilled to achieve progress beyond all expectation, not only for nerve problems, but other serious health problems too. Undoubtedly this system is linked to the brain which is the indirect master of every function of the body from blood pressure to heart rate and immune response to hormones. Personally I feel that the innate energy within us, which has the power to heal, comes from the immune system. I am often surprised to see how the immune system plays a major role in restoration of the Life Force.

I will relate to the "I am" diagram, reproduced here, in several chapters of the book.

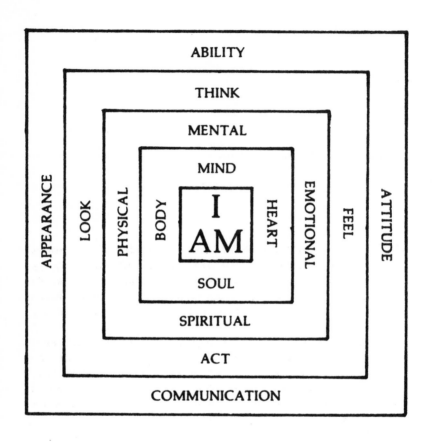

2

Stress

STRESS IS undoubtedly an "in" word these days. Everyone is talking about their daily dose of stress. Harassed mothers moan about being unable to cope with their unruly flock; businessmen are caught up in the rat race; and even today's children lead high-powered lives. So it is not surprising that stress has become a major talking point.

I believe, however, that although discussed more than ever before, stress-related problems have been with us since the beginning. Everything is relative, after all. The caveman who couldn't track down his dinner probably suffered from stress as much as the young housewife rushing round the supermarket searching for ingredients for a special meal.

Let's be honest, life without stress would be boring. In fact, in some circumstances a certain amount of stress is beneficial. It is when stress becomes excessive or prolonged that the trouble starts. Stress is common to everyone but some of us can cope better than others when things start to get out of hand. Everyone, however, is capable of learning how to control stress and channel it into positive energy.

Many psychologists and stress groups try to gauge a person's "stress count" by using scores from one to a hundred for a variety of situations likely to induce stress. The highest scores were given for the death of someone close, divorce, unemployment, moving house, coping with illness, domestic problems, sex difficulties, and, believe it or not, success in life. Yes, it is often the most successful people, in terms of financial reward and achievements at work, who become so stressed that illness forces them to pull in their reins. In spite of growing prosperity for many, dissatisfaction with life generally is quite common. If we have a son, we want a daughter; if we have a good income, we want a bigger income; if we have satisfactory health, we want even better health. It is a tiny minority who are content with what they have got. Most of us want more, more, more . . .

This strong desire to do better is one which I have noticed on my travels throughout the world, even among the less fortunate and this, in itself, is very good. My experience of people who suffer tremendous stress has taught me that they have stretched themselves to the limit. Many are very ill before they call a halt to their fast-living. We must learn to accept life and take it a day at a time for our health's sake.

In Britain, where recently unemployment has been rife, stress is on the rampage. A person who is bored and frustrated is just as prone to stress problems as someone with not enough free time. People either accept or don't accept unemployment. Those who do accept it try to make the best of their situation and channel any negative feelings or emotions into new activities. The result of this attitude is very often a better job than the one previously held. The other person mopes around the house all day feeling tensed-up, nervous and depressed. Excessive stress has him in such a strong grip that he can do nothing except complain about his sad situation.

It is the latter type which I come across most in my work because they can be susceptible to the growing problems of high blood pressure, stomach ulcers, migraines, eczema, asthma, mental disorders, and, some researchers believe, cancer. Stress is high on the suspect list also for inducing young people to adopt bad habits like smoking, drinking, and over-eating, which in turn bring about more disease.

We can, however, avoid stress. In fact, it is quite amazing what a positive attitude can do. All too often we fail to acknowledge that our mind operates in various dimensions. If we accept any situation we are placed in, we can escape from many problems. We are then in a position to make the best of the situation and exert favourable influence over it; in other words, to use it to our advantage. There is always light at the end of the tunnel and if we think positively our immune system is triggered and the Life Force becomes so strong that the body can throw off stress.

Two extreme cases come to mind. A clergyman came to see me in a highly-stressed state. Not only was the poor man's financial position bad, but he had a string of other problems which had reduced him to what we term a "nervous wreck". He had lost faith in himself and also partially in the One about whom he was preaching. I discovered that he had accepted his stressed state to a point where there was almost no getting through to him. Eventually I had to be rude to shake him out of this acceptance. I asked him whether he thought his mind was stronger than his body, or the contrary. He immediately replied that the mind was the stronger.

As the "I am" diagram shows, the mind influences our mental state which then affects our thinking and consequently this controls our ability. So if we influence our minds positively we will get a desirable result in whatever we are doing. The clergyman had let his body speak. This influenced his physical body by making him feel drained. The evidence of this was in his appearance which, when I met him first, was pretty grim. I told him that the mind was so strong that if I sat in the corner and told my big toe it was very painful, I would experience pain. If we influence the mind positively, I explained, our ability to cope with stress will be much greater. He apparently understood this theory but I realised that I had not quite hit the nail on the head.

I plunged ahead and asked him why he was in such a tizzy about flesh and bones when he believed in eternal life for the spirit. My words shook him but that was exactly what I had planned and, thereafter, I made great progress in helping him to achieve a positive outlook. After three visits he was a changed person and our relationship had developed into a good friendship.

Stress-related problems range from the mild to the severe and in some cases, as in the second of my extreme cases, the fuse has blown and psychosis and neurosis are a great possibility.

The patient was a very neurotic man who worked for me many years ago. His family life loaded much stress on to his shoulders and he had become almost useless as an employee. I wanted to help him, however, and thought carefully about how I would go about it. One morning I told my assistant to tell this employee, soon after his arrival at work, that he looked awful. I then told another of his colleagues to say immediately upon greeting him that he looked desperately ill. As it happened, I was first to meet him that morning and I asked him what the matter was. "Nothing today, I feel fine," he replied. Half an hour later, after he had bumped into my accomplices, he rushed into my office proclaiming that he had looked in the mirror feeling very ill all of a sudden. My plan had worked. His brain had absorbed what he had heard from others. Consequently, his mental state had been influenced and he believed he was ill. I sent him home, told him to call the doctor and said I would visit him later that afternoon. When I saw him we had a heart-to-heart talk which opened his eyes a great deal and he agreed to follow my advice on how to cope with stress. For a long time this man had been absorbed in his own problems, building them up out of all proportion. I was forced to use a method which showed him how silly he really was. Soon he was one of my best employees.

People who have too much of everything — money, possessions and opportunity for example — are prone to stress.

A charming young couple from Holland came into this category of people. They simply arrived at the door of my clinic one day saying they had come for a rest. I was reluctant to believe this because I knew they could get more than enough rest at home, and I soon realised that they desperately wanted to change their stressful lifestyle.

I learned that they were fighting with each other constantly and life, for both of them, had become unbearable. Not long ago, eight years to the day they turned up on the doorstep, I received a lovely letter from them telling me how contented they were with life. All those years ago I had talked to them about the real values of life and encouraged them to take up voluntary work to help the underprivileged. This they had enjoyed. They said it helped them to attach new meaning to life. I managed to stop them smoking, to reduce their heavy drinking, and persuaded them to adopt a healthier diet. Finally, I convinced them of the need for a little exercise.

When God created man, I told them, he was like a lifeless body, just a conglomeration of cells. God then started to charge the body and poured into it the breath of life. Thus man became conscious, began to breathe, to feel, and a living soul was created.

After I had taught them how to minimise stress, I told them of one of my most valuable remedies for restoring the Life Force when we have allowed our minds and bodies to become imbalanced. I related the story of how, many years ago, when working in a hospital, I had met a young doctor who was able to perform more operations than any of her colleagues and still look fresh and relaxed at the end of the day. I asked her what her secret was and she replied that all she did was try to breathe correctly in order to have an energy supply to draw on whenever needed. She explained that although her method was simple, it still required a bit of understanding.

Where does a new-born baby breathe? You will find that there is little movement of the chest and there is a rhythmic rise and fall slightly under the navel. As the child grows older and forms its own personality, this breathing pattern will change, usually rising from the navel upwards. Tense people tend to breathe high up in the chest and the same can be said for those suffering from asthma.

The young doctor then told me that her breathing technique was based on "Hara" and to this day I am grateful that I managed to take a short course in this method of correct breathing. There are obviously too many exercises to mention here but I would like to tell you about one which I practise most days.

About four o'clock in the afternoon, the time I was born, I sometimes begin to feel a little tired. This, by the way, is an experience which many people feel when the time of their birth approaches. I lie on the floor when I feel tired and tell myself to relax completely. My eyes are closed and I tell every part of my body, from top to toe, to relax until I feel as if I am sinking deeper and deeper into the floor. Then I place my left hand about half an inch beneath my navel and put the other hand on it. At that point, a magnetic ring on the vital centre of man — "Hara" — has been formed. The Chinese have an old saying that the navel is the gate to all happiness and certainly, by doing this, one feels very relaxed. Next I breathe in slowly through the nose, filling my stomach with air and keeping the rib cage still. This sounds easier than it is and actually takes a little time to master properly.

Concentrate your mind on your stomach and breathe in slowly. Once the stomach is filled with air, round your lips and slowly breathe out pulling the stomach flat. This can be done as often as desired. Normally, the sensation after finishing this exercise is either one of complete relaxation and the desire for a nice sleep, or of refreshment and the desire to return to work. I must stress that it should be performed naturally, as a baby would do it. Sometimes it helps to imagine yourself walking in a beautiful garden where you discover the wonderful scent of roses which you inhale slowly.

I told my young couple that I once knew óf a director of a large firm. Now and again, when he attended important meetings, he found himself making excuses to go to the toilet so he could practise "Hara" to relieve his stress and tension.

Personally-speaking, I always find that it increases my energy flow dramatically and I am surprised at how therapeutic it is. It doesn't even take much time. I have recommended this method to many patients who have come to me suffering from stress. I have seen it help to restore the Life Force which then helps the body to respond when treated as a whole. Of course, we all know that out of stress a lot of other problems are born. These I will discuss in the following chapters.

3

Fears

MY FATHER often said to me: "Fear can be one's worst enemy."
I must say, however, that in the course of my work I have often
found that fear can also be a good friend.

On the other hand, whenever a person's life is ruled by fear,
there is something far wrong. If a negative fear has taken over
your life, you are not alone. In all of my practices I have
encountered numerous extreme cases of negative fear.

The first page of one of the psychology books which I studied
at college said that intuition makes us want to run away if a
fearful experience crosses our path. Another book said that fear
was a left-over from the days when we lived in the jungle and felt
afraid if a wild animal was after our blood. That may be true but
in today's world we have other problems concerning fear which
must be tackled.

As well as negative fears there are positive fears. No one could
argue that it is wrong, for instance, to take great precautions
before attempting something which involves an element of
danger. For example, fear of falling and fear of unexpected noise
are positive fears. There are hundreds of negative fears, the
most common being of sleepless nights, of getting cancer, of
death, of the future, of not being able to swallow, of dreams, of
stuttering, of being impotent, of darkness, of losing friends, of
ill-health, and even of success.

The fears of patients who come to me are mainly rooted in past experience and in such cases it often takes quite some time to actually discover what the real fear is. Whatever an individual's fear may be, there is one thing which can be of tremendous help; quite simply to share the fear with a friend or relative.

Negative fear is a terrible enemy and where it exists there is little chance of harmony between mind and body. Indeed it tends to block all positive relationships.

A young Irish girl consulted me in my former Birmingham clinic some years ago. She was married and had a lovely child. Before she spoke a single word, she burst into tears. After this release of emotion she calmed down and we started talking. She looked like a little shocked bird and it was not easy to extract information from her. I learned that during her childhood she had lived through some disturbing and highly emotional experiences. Her fear was that such traumas would be repeated and she therefore was afraid of fear itself.

Dr Bach's "Rescue Remedy" lived up to its name when I turned to it in this case. I always make sure my cupboards contain this excellent composition of Cherry Plum, Clematis, Impatiens, Rock Rose and Star of Bethlehem. As well as advising the Irish colleen to take this remedy, I tried to give her some positive advice on how to tackle her everyday problems. Three months later, when I saw her again, she had changed dramatically and was a completely different girl. No longer was she haunted by her unfortunate past. I asked her what she had experienced on returning home after her first visit to me. Her simple but honest answer was that the remedy had soothed her troubled mind and that she had taken great care to remember my words of advice. I had told her that before she could even start to tackle her fears, she had to first recognise them. Remembering this, she had kept telling herself that the key to freedom of fear was in her own hands.

When a patient discovers exactly what he or she is afraid of, and shares the problem with someone else, freedom from fear is just round the corner. Often all that is then needed is some homoeopathic treatment or even acupuncture, and by taking these steps, even the most horrible fears can be overcome.

I remember a young woman who approached me after a lecture I gave in Glasgow at a meeting in aid of Cancer Research.

She told me that she was in the middle of a divorce because of her dreadful fear of cancer. She had been haunted by this for 12 years and it had destroyed the quality of her married life.

I told her about a lecture I attended once in London, given by a famous French professor. The subject of her lecture was cancer and at the end of it a woman in the audience asked if she could put a question on the disease. "Why do you want to ask a question?" asked the professor. The reply was: "Because I have cancer." The professor then reacted in an extraordinary way and said: "Never use the word cancer again." She then told the woman that every time the word cancer was to pass her lips, her problem would worsen. The professor's message was that it is wrong to influence the mind negatively. After this was understood by the questioner, who was herself a doctor of medicine, the professor answered her question without once using the forbidden word.

My young woman had been assured by her doctor that she didn't have cancer and I asked her why she doubted his word. From her answer I realised that she was using cancer as an excuse for another quite different fear which ruled her life. I advised her to take Dr Bach's Clematis and, when I met her next, she described herself as a stupid fool for having allowed this fear to give her so much misery.

As a young child I found myself facing many fearful experiences, mainly resulting from the Second World War, and I learned at a young age how to tackle the problem of fear positively.

I like to tell this story because it trained me to overcome fear by faith. My father was taken away by the Germans and my brother deported to their country. My mother was left with the task of looking after, not only me, but a great many others who were in need. I will never forget how scared I was that the Germans would get hold of my mother and kill her, until we had an experience which strengthened our faith. The door-bell rang one evening and on the doorstep stood a man wearing a clog on one foot and a shoe on the other. He told my mother that the Germans were after him and asked for refuge in our home. He explained that he had escaped from a ship which was to deport him to a concentration camp.

My mother allowed him to come in. The first thing she did was to find a herbal ointment to treat his scabies. This was no problem to her because knowledge of herbal treatments runs in her family. She then helped him hide beneath the floorboards. I could see that she was worried for he was not the only one hiding in our house.

Not long after, we heard the Germans coming and realised they were searching houses and carrying out spot-checks. Anxiously, my mother expressed her fears to me. "All we can do now is pray that we will be protected," she said. Our prayers were answered. Every house in the street was turned over except ours. As soon as the coast was clear my mother told me that I would now know how to overcome fear in my future life. It was like a miracle because we knew that the Germans were not likely to forget or to make a mistake. We were saved and I had learned what a marvellous thing faith is for tackling fear.

I must admit though, that I am still surprised when faith proves to be a wonderful friend for persons on their death-bed. If the end of life is a struggle, there are remedies which can help. In one such case I used Dr Vogel's Ignatia which takes the fear of death away. I also give this remedy to people who are mourning the death of a loved one. It works almost instantly and it is marvellous that there are such remedies which can soften the suffering of sorrow.

Here again, however, a positive mind is a great help. I was amazed at the strength of one man who was dying but refused to accept it. In hospital he noticed that every time someone died he was moved a bit nearer to the door of the ward. When he reached the bed nearest to the door of the ward, he sat up and proclaimed: "I don't want to die yet." He didn't and was still going strong four years later.

There is another fear which I have seen over and over again in Holland and elsewhere, but to which little attention is paid. This is a shame because Fear of Man can be quite disastrous.

A young couple came to see me and on their first visit I realised that they had some real problems. For a start their marriage had fallen by the wayside because of some serious mishaps in the husband's life. They were a very religious couple and the man told me that he was so ashamed of bits of his past that he was terrified of meeting anyone he knew in the street. He wished he could carry his home on his back like a snail so he could crawl into it if he spotted a familiar face. This type of problem is one I have met often. In this particular case I knew it had to be approached from a spiritual point of view. I thought of my diagram, and realised that his soul was going through a crisis which had affected him spiritually, resulting in feelings of overwhelming guilt. Consequently, his communication with his wife, indeed with anyone, was practically non-existent. While he was talking I was thinking of our highly-respected Queen Beatrix of Holland. After her coronation she was asked which king or queen from the past she had most admired. Her immediate reply was King David of biblical days.

I don't think there was ever a king who went through so many emotional traumas as King David. Not only did he have some fearful experiences, he also had to learn to overcome guilt. I told the young couple that King David would never have left us with so rich an inheritance of experience if he had not gone through such traumas. King David asked the "King of Kings" to be washed from his sins with the herbal remedy, Hyssop. This remedy has some wonderful health-restoring properties and in many Eastern countries is used as a natural antibiotic. In the Western world it is used to stabilise blood pressure. Even over 3000 years ago, King David must have known of the cleansing and healing effects of this mysterious herbal remedy.

I told the husband who was suffering guilt, that once King David learned to live with his regrettable experiences, his life became of far greater value and he was able to help other people. I drew the couple's attention to the treasure of wisdom which King David left behind. The story helped the troubled husband to overcome his fear of man and some time later I received a letter from him saying that life for them both had taken on a totally new meaning.

Whatever your fear might be, you must always try to look to the future because, as said already, most fears are rooted in the past.

One evening just as I was finishing a hard day's work, two girls rang my door-bell. One of them looked so shattered that I felt I had to devote some time to her. I learned that she had tried to commit suicide three times. On the third attempt she had thrown herself in the river. "Unfortunately, someone noticed and saved me," she said. During a long chat I discovered that she had been through three abortions in quite a short time, and had damaged her health with some dreadful habits involving the use of drugs. Eventually, after much probing, I discovered that she was scared of her father, a high-ranking police officer. She stayed with her friend in Scotland for a few weeks which allowed me to help re-build her health. I told her she should tackle her father without fear and talk to him sensibly. She managed to overcome her fear and family communication was restored. This done, her problems dissolved. She is now a happily married mother.

I have great sympathy also for another common fear, that suffered by young people when exams are looming ahead. Sometimes it is the actual exams they fear but equally likely to incite fear are the mother and father who are keen for their offspring to achieve top marks. Pressure in these circumstances only leads to more fear and often results in exam failures which could have been avoided.

My very last exam was an oral and I knew that everything depended on the kind of impression I made on the Government representative who had difficult questions ready to fire at me. This, though, was not the only reason for my apprehension. As a youth I was often teased because I was small in height. I was almost obsessive about it. I was very self-conscious, therefore, about meeting this important man. Fortunately, the previous day I had learned another lesson from nature, one which was to help me in my face-to-face meeting with the examiner. I had been staying, with the intention of doing some last minute exam preparations with my aunt and uncle near Amsterdam. I worked through my books that afternoon, sitting outside in the sunshine, until, at about three o'clock, the weather took a turn for the worse. The sky looked menacing and, as the clouds gathered in the distance, I heard the rumble of thunder. The lovely sunny afternoon was changing into a dark and dismal evening. Several times I had broken my concentration to look at a most beautiful water lily in the pond. As I quickly gathered up my books, I remembered the lily and went over to see it for the last time that day. I was just in time to see the flower closing its petals as the rumblings of distant thunder grew louder. I didn't mind getting wet as I realised that the rain could do nothing to damage the delicate inner beauty of the lily.

This simple act of nature restored my confidence and I realised that all I could do was to sell myself as well as possible. If necessary, I could protect the inner me from the outside world. My new-found philosophy worked. Of the eight people who sat the exam that day only two succeeded and the Government representative congratulated me for being the youngest candidate in Holland ever to have passed.

I was lucky, for I quickly learned to control my obsession about height. When fears become obsessions it is very worrying. They need immediate attention because they can lead to much more serious problems.

In life the two most important emotions we experience are love and fear. Love is our natural inheritance but fear is something which the mind invents. In other words, it is generated in the mind. When life generally is not going too well there is always a temptation to live in the future. This temptation must be avoided. There is nothing more beneficial for the soul than taking each day as it comes and tackling our work and our relationships with fellow human-beings in the spirit of love.

We must remember that it is impossible to experience love and fear at the same time. A very good piece of biblical advice was given by a man who had experienced fear in his life. He said: "There is no fear in love and perfect love casts out fear."

4

Anxiety

MANY PEOPLE spend more than half of their lives feeling anxious. Anxiety, like tension or phobias, is the result of excessive stress. An anxious person, in other words, has an uneasy mind and when this uneasiness is recognised and understood, it can quite easily be controlled. It is simple to say "why worry?" to an anxious person. Too often people are told, "just forget your worries", or, as I sometimes find myself saying, "throw them in the bucket". This attitude, however, is not the answer.

An anxious person should be treated with patience and understanding. Handled this way, the sufferer is more willing to spill out worries and this is the first step towards recovery.

Sometimes, of course, anxiety is not a bad thing. It triggers off the flow of adrenalin which alerts all our senses to danger and can help us face and tackle problems. For instance, it can help athletes and public speakers give first-class performances.

Feeling anxious and growing excited are very similar feelings which have very different implications. We must learn to recognise the emotion we are experiencing and this can be done by acknowledging signals emitted by the body.

How do we know we are anxious? Perhaps we are more active than usual and unable to settle for long, and maybe the extra energy we are expending is making us feel extremely tired. One thing is sure, anxiety is often misunderstood. Frequently people tell me they are depressed or suffering from a specific health problem and usually it does not take me long to discover that they are, in fact, experiencing anxiety because it is quite common for anxiety to manifest itself in physical symptoms.

Pay attention to the signals given out by your body. It is surprising how many ways it can indicate the presence of anxiety — lightheadedness, headaches, backache, dry mouth, butterflies in the tummy, sweating hands, weak legs, feeling of faintness.

A patient who consulted me years ago said she had severe heart problems. On checking her medical records, I noticed that she had no history of such problems and was, in fact, very healthy. Nevertheless, her symptoms did suggest that her theory was right. When I saw her in the waiting room of my clinic on the first few occasions she consulted me, I could see for myself that she had broken out in a sweat, had terrible palpitations, and was complaining of a pain in her chest. Her doctor told her that she was just nervous but after talking to her for a while I discovered that she was suffering from a nervous anxiety. Fortunately, I was able to successfully treat her and every time I see her now she reminds me that the most important factor in her treatment was recognising her problem and knowing that her heart was strong.

Anxiety is also the cause of common problems like nail-biting and lip-chewing. Such habits are merely a symptom of underlying uneasiness which must be brought to the surface. This done, it is much easier to control these habits. Acupuncture can also be of great help here.

Why do we get anxious? I feel that the media, especially television and magazines, have a lot to answer for. Nervous children are prone to negative reactions after watching or reading about something which upsets them.

I remember a family I treated in my Preston clinic. They lived in a sprawling housing scheme and one of the children was very anxious. She had seen a terrifying scene on a television programme and it had left a lasting impression on her. At the bus stop, waiting for the school bus each morning, she clung desperately to her mother, fearing that a similar danger was coming her way. Frequently she trembled all over and was just a sad and pathetic child.

The first time I met her I was slightly taken aback by the shocked expression permanently on her face. I also realised that she was a frustrated youngster and it took me quite a while to find out why. Eventually I learned from her about the incident in the television programme and knew that she was anticipating a similar horrifying incident happening in her own life. After discussing her fearful state I gave her a remedy for her nervous system which calmed her down and allowed me to help her further. I have since met her, years later, and she is now a self-confident happy young woman and a far cry from the frightened child she once was.

Something which adults can do much easier than children, is question their anxiety. Why do I get tense? Why do I behave nervously? Why do I worry? These are questions which should be asked and once the answers are found, a method of treatment can be selected.

A treatment which I often advise for anxiety is the relaxation method. Sit down on an easy chair with your head resting and your feet flat on the floor. Breathe calmly and listen to your breath going in and out. Now take a very deep breath and, when expiring, say to yourself "relax". Do this three times. Then say to yourself over and over again, "I can do it", thinking of whatever your problem may be, picturing yourself going to the shops, or boarding an aeroplane. You must convince yourself that you can do it. When you have finished creating this mental picture, pat yourself on the back for having done so well. Breathe deeply three times and open your eyes.

Do this exercise three times a day — when you wake up, at lunchtime, and before sleeping at night. Practise it in a quiet room and try never to skip an exercise. What you are doing is putting a new programme into the computer. Be patient, it may take up to six months before it starts working.

I know first-hand about anxiety because as a child I suffered considerable anxiety, mainly because part of my childhood took place in wartime. I remember my fear that we would be killed in the bombings but I also remember an important lesson I learned at that time. My mother was helping out in the most dangerous area of Holland — Arnhem-Oosterbeek. During one of the air raids an old gentleman took me into his room where he had an old-fashioned three-dimensional viewer. I was so intrigued that I failed to hear the bombs and was completely oblivious to any danger. The moral of this story is that if we can concentrate on something interesting, we will not be afraid of imminent danger.

Fear has a very significant role to play in anxiety, for the dictionary tells us that anxiety is a neurosis in which fear and apprehension control the patient's behaviour and ideas.

For many years now I have treated a lecturer for his neck problems. Whenever the problem rears its painful head, a little manipulation solves it. I noticed, one day, however, that his general behaviour was becoming very nervous and he was growing anxious. I knew that he had next-door-neighbour problems at home and decided to warn him not to let himself get bogged down with concern about this. I learned that he didn't want help and was not too surprised when I heard he had experienced a nervous breakdown. After three months of trying to battle on alone, he came back to me with his tail between his legs and we managed to dig down to the roots and pull out the trouble.

Basically, his problem was a fairly minor one which had been triggered off as a result of experiences he had many years ago. As a child he had a problem with a neighbour of his parents. Whenever he met this particular neighbour he was told how stupid his hairstyle looked. Consequently he had a complex about his hair. Luckily we nipped his fear in the bud before he became very phobic about it.

This reminds me of a famous musician I once treated in London. She came to me when she was at the peak of her career because she had developed a phobia about something which happened when she was a child of four. Someone had tried to interfere with her sexually. This, of course, was a great shock and she vividly remembered screaming in fear, although she did not dare to tell her mother about the incident. It took me a long time to extract from her exactly what had happened at this tender age. I treated her with homoeopathy, acupuncture and some other remedies and, fortunately, she broke free from her phobia. Otherwise it could have been the early curtailment of a very successful and glittering career.

We often find that gifted people, especially those in the fields of art and music, experience great frustration as a result of their exceptional talent. This can easily lead to stress, anxieties, and worse still, phobias.

It is very sad when a phobia is allowed to demean a person's life but it does regularly happen. There are many people who consult me because they don't want to join their husbands at receptions or dinners, or because they are terrified of birds or small animals, or even because they are terrified of hair. In fact, there are hundreds of different phobias. The most common one though, is agoraphobia, a neurotic fear of open spaces, perhaps of being in a field, standing at the bus stop, or in a lonely or busy place.

I feel very sorry for people with such a phobia because they miss out on life so much. Many never seek help although this problem can sometimes be relieved. Too often I hear people saying, "This is my problem and I have to live with it." This, of course, is nonsense. If you have a problem you must fight to overcome it. You don't have to live with it forever.

Another common phobia is acrophobia, a morbid fear of heights. This is one I hear about frequently in my clinic, and an unfortunate one because it is a phobia which takes a tremendous lot of pleasure away from life. Not long ago I spoke to a charming lady who dearly wished she could visit her family abroad. The only travel possibility was the aeroplane but she had a tremendous fear of heights and and couldn't bear the thought of flying.

I told her that she could be helped by acupuncture but was quickly told that she also had a dread for needles. Undeterred, I showed her the needles which drew a favourable response. "Is that all?" she asked, adding that she thought they would be enormous frightening instruments. I then told her that flying was even less fearful and almost immediately she said she was willing to undergo acupuncture because her fears were lessening. After the treatment she felt confident enought to tackle anything and, two days later, left Turnhouse Airport feeling on top of the world — literally! I was delighted when I received a postcard from her telling me how much she had enjoyed her flight.

On my travels around the world I have seen many people who share this fear of flying. They always benefit from a few words of encouragement, as well as some homeopathic remedies. I remember so well the last time I visited Toronto. My conquest was the CN Tower, the highest in the world. After reaching the dizzy heights of the top of the tower, I was stepping out of the lift when I met my old friend, Dr John Christopher, the world-renowned herbalist. He looked wisely at the people with pale faces who obviously wanted to go to the very top, but couldn't because they were afraid, and said to me: "You know, there are some wonderful herbal remedies to give to these people who would really like to go up but don't dare."

Another common phobia is simply termed a social phobia. This was what held back one of my patients who was an excellent public speaker until he became aware of all the people listening to him. After getting off to a flying start he would suddenly notice the intensely interested faces staring at him and clam up. It was so bad that he found himself totally tongue-tied and able to say nothing more. All he could do was end his speech abruptly and sit down. Fortunately I was able to help him through acupuncture and autogenic training.

But a bigger problem than the social phobia is that of claustrophobia, a fear of confined spaces, like a small room. During wartime we were frequently forced to go down into the cellars and sit for hours in the enclosed oppressive atmosphere. Later on in life I found myself terrified of going into a lift or a small shop, but I managed to overcome this fear by talking to myself positively and repeating continually that there was nothing to be afraid of.

It is possible, whatever the phobia or anxiety, for a sufferer to return to normal if the problem is tackled the right way. The origin of the phobia is not really of any consequence and it is often a bad idea to reflect on this. Many patients see the problem as an illness and ask themselves: "Am I going mad?" or "Am I mentally ill?" Nothing could be further from the truth. Such problems can start after traumatic experiences like illness, divorce, long periods of stress, and a bad marriage.

After recognising the problem the first step to take is to ensure that a good balanced diet is being eaten and that protein intake is low. Animal proteins especially should be minimised or cut out altogether. There will be more information on the subject of diet in a further chapter. Plenty of rest, exercise and sleep are also essential and joining a group to gain the support of others with similar problems can be invaluable. Group situations can also be a great help to the concentration, a lack of which is usually observed in sufferers of any problem related to the nervous system. Psychologically acute and prolonged feelings of anxiety always divert the concentration and when this occurs there is a need for the mind to be re-trained. The simple methods of exercise outlined in chapter one are excellent in such cases.

Earlier this year I dealt with a patient whose concentration had taken a severe blow. He was a very eminent diplomat, a very respected man, and as a result of a heated debate among foreign delegates at an important conference, had suffered a heart attack. He fought it most admirably and was able to return to his demanding job, only to find that his concentration had weakened and this had affected his memory. When I saw how determined he was to overcome the anxious feelings which had impaired his powers of concentration, I was most encouraged. I felt confident that it would be easy to treat this man because of the conscious effort he was making to overcome his present condition.

In such conditions the herbal remedy, Vinca Minor, can give tremendous results. Like all herbal remedies it is free from side-effects and one can take it without the risk of becoming "hooked". Anxieties and phobias should never be tackled with drugs. They provide only temporary relief and very often only make the problem worse.

In nature's garden there are plenty of helpful remedies. Certainly, drugs such as tranquillers and alcohol have the ability to alleviate the situation but we must realise, that under their influence, we cannot function effectively in our work or domestic life. After only short periods of taking drugs physical dependence or addiction can result. Consequent withdrawal symptoms are always severe and occasionally fatal.

A patient whom I am treating just now is a victim of drugs. She is completely dependent on drugs and is practically blind to her problem. Every time she comes to see me she faints after a few minutes. Her brain cells have really taken a beating and it will take a lot of persuasion, understanding and patience to slowly reduce her drug intake so that she can enjoy life once more.

Every anxiety or phobia in an individual has its own characteristics and must be treated on this basis. There are, however, several methods of treatment which are of general help including relaxation, acupuncture, homoeopathy, aromatherapy, herbal and flower therapy, and autogenic training. These apart, there is something which is a marvellous treatment — a double dose of sympathy and understanding. Never tell someone to pull themselves together. These words can only aggravate the situation. People who suffer in this way have nothing to be ashamed of and self-help is their best bet to reach the road to recovery. Once they are on this road they will still need loads of praise and encouragement. "You can do it!"

5

Depression

"I FEEL GHASTLY. I've even thought of committing suicide. I'm so desperately lonely. I just want to hide away from everything. My moods are so changeable that sometimes I think I must be some kind of Jekyll and Hyde. Please, please help me!"

These are only some of the expressions I hear every day. They are the plaintive cries for help from people, who, for various reasons have become the victims of depression, an illness which is becoming more and more prevalent as the pressures of life build up in our modern society.

Depression is probably one of the most unpleasant experiences a person can go through. Usually it is much more difficult to endure than a physical illness, yet sufferers are often treated with impatience. They are told bluntly to "pull themselves together", but this is the worst possible advice because it is precisely what they are so desperately trying to do — without success. What is often dismissed as "just depression" is a serious illness which induces feelings of utter hopelessness leading to a total lack of interest in life and feelings of utter worthlessness.

There are various kinds of depression. The two main ones are endogenous and exogenous. The first results from hormonal and biochemical changes within the body. The second is influenced by outside factors.

It is very often difficult to differentiate between stress,

anxiety and depression, because in all of these problems the emotions play a big part. There is no doubt, though, that faulty diet — an imbalance of nutrients, vitamins, trace elements and enzymes — plays a major role in any depressive illness. People with allergies, sensitivities to certain foods, and hypoglycaemia, for example, are therefore more susceptible to depression, and it is a proven fact that there can be a quick change for the better in someone who is depressed, if dietary supplements are taken and eating habits are improved. Indeed, the first step I usually take in the treatment of depression is to change the diet of the sufferer. The body is so often crying out for vitamins and supplements.

This form of treatment is supported by extensive investigations carried out by the National Research Council in America who have dossiers containing proof of success. They have shown that, even for schizophrenia, which very often results from depression, a good balanced diet can work wonders.

It is very important to realise that the sooner a person escapes from any of these problems associated with depression, the better, and luckily there are many ways of throwing off the chains of dejection. For example, relaxation, meditation and visualisation can be of great help, while plenty of exercise and the discovery of new interests are also invaluable. The key to recovery lies within us all and we must help ourselves to find it.

Quite often the victims of depression try to break out of the "straightjacket" by resorting to drugs like anti-depressants and alcohol. These may bring temporary relief but they are never the answer. They only help to diminish our feelings of responsibility to our bodies and are invariably followed by even deeper feelings of hopelessness and despair.

It is always advisable to seek professional help for the treatment of depression and it should always be remembered that it is dangerous to stop taking pills abruptly without the knowledge of the doctor who prescribed them.

I have tried over and over again to explain to people how important it is for them to re-discover a feeling of responsibility for their own bodies and on this score I have no doubt that every good doctor or specialist will be only too willing to help sufferers of depression to reduce their drug intake.

I remember the case of a man who, unbelievably, took 60

tablets of a well-known drug every day as a treatment for depression. He was a bachelor and the root of his problem was a common one — the "mother and son" complex, known to psychiatrists as the "Oedipus Complex". The amount of drugs he was taking shocked me and, after his blood tests were analysed, it was clear that his health, especially his liver, was already in great danger. He was begging for help. At work he was incapable of carrying out his job, and his condition had deteriorated after the specialist he consulted had called him a "junkie". In fact, he was desperate.

I immediately put him on to a special diet and gave him a good dose of Vitamin B3 as well as Neuroforce from Dr Vogel. This enabled me to reduce his intake of drugs by ten capsules a day in the first fortnight of treatment. He was the type of person who was receptive to meditation and I encouraged him to practise this. He followed my advice and began slowly to regain the confidence he had lost. When I saw him recently he told me he had fully recovered, was back at work and pulling more than his weight.

In my first interview with him he told me that I would never be able to help him. I countered this remark by saying that I understood his problem and that he could depend on me to do my very best. I saw that he believed me. He co-operated admirably and this was the reason why we both saw such good results. He had a smile on his face when I saw him last. His dark gloomy look had disappeared and he even said he felt that his physical health had improved. I told him that it takes seventy-two muscles to frown and only fourteen to smile, and reminded him to keep smiling.

Orthodox medicine has often doubted the view that stress and depression can make a person more prone to infections, germs and viruses, but I saw this quite clearly in a girl who was sent to me by her doctor. When I did an iridology test on her I found that her liver had been badly affected. I asked her what happened. She said that for a long time she had suffered a great deal of emotional stress. I could only conclude that a virus had taken advantage of this situation and wormed its way into her liver, making it impossible for the organ to function normally.

She responded immediately when I helped her poor liver by putting her on a special diet containing a lot of artichokes. Next I gave her a massive dose of Echinacea which does a wonderful job as a natural antibiotic. Her depression started to lift, her health improved and within three visits she was as right as rain.

One of the best friends the liver has is oxygen. As Dr Vogel said so clearly in his book *The Liver – Regulator of our Health*, the liver has some dangerous enemies, including alcohol, nicotine and excesses of fat. It functions like the most efficient laboratory in the world filtering one thousand two hundred pints of blood every twenty-four hours.

This brings to mind the case of a man who held a well-respected job. He was very suicidal when he came to me and said he had been forced into coming. I joked with him and asked if he had come because he wanted to be helped or because he wanted me to help him commit suicide. That broke the ice a bit and he told me there had been quite a number of suicides in his family. He said that life was meaningless and that he too wished he could end it all. I enquired about how he was coping at work and discovered that there, in a position of authority, he felt fine. The terrible depressive moods came over him when he was alone at home.

I asked him if the clouds of depression gathered just after he had smoked "goodness knows how many" cigarettes or cigars, and consumed a considerable amount of whisky. He replied with a question. Did I have second sight? I explained that it was the result of years of experience which made me able to identify his problem so quickly. I believe the liver is involved in this kind of depression, although I must say I have often been criticised for making such a statement. I do, however, have evidence. When I treat this nicotine and alcohol induced depression with acupuncture, I go straight to the liver points and always get positive reactions.

After a few weeks this once suicidal man reported that he was a lot happier. This was the result of paying a little extra attention to his diet, reducing his smoking and drinking, acupuncture, and some good liver-cleansing remedies. Soon he was completely free of the dark depression he had once endured and although I treated him a long time ago, he still writes to me now and again.

Degenerative diseases, very often induced by stress, can result in toxaemia and high blood viscosity. In such cases there is often a reduced oxygen supply to the tissues. This is the reason why positive results are usually obtained with hyperbaric oxygen treatment.

I have often been mystified by how acupuncture and visualisation programmes can bring about a reversal of certain diseases and this makes me feel sure that, like energy, oxygen has a great role to play in the medicine of the future. We see this with the depressed person who is drinking heavily. The oxygen flow to the tissue cells is decreased and this has an influence on the triglycerides, cholesterol and blood viscosity. It upsets the hormonal balance, attacks the immune system, and decreases the lymphocytes and white cells.

In this situation depression becomes a state of disease, causing physical debilitation which leads in turn to body degeneration. On the other hand, understandably, hypoglycaemia sufferers can be easily depressed and taking the wrong kind of food and drink only makes the problem worse. When blood sugar is low a person begins to feel tired and confused. Vision can be blurred and interest in the world around ebbs.

I remember a very distressed young woman who came to me. She had been this way for a number of years and eventually had written to a specialist in London about her problem. He asked her if she had ever thought that she had hypoglycaemia and advised her to consult me. It was almost miraculous how quickly her condition changed after I made radical changes in her diet and prescribed evening primrose oil capsules. Without further assistance she was back to normal within six weeks.

She had told me that her basic problem was the way her character could change in a matter of seconds, leading her to suspect she was some kind of "Jekyll and Hyde". One minute she could be full of fun, the next a morose, gloomy and unco-operative character. Her husband and other relatives just couldn't understand her and the sudden switches of mood had created much family friction. She was yet another example of how necessary it is with all forms of depression to alter one's lifestyle.

I admired a doctor who was greatly loved by his patients. He was the type of person who makes an excellent doctor and he appeared to have everything going for him. Yet when he consulted me he was in great despair simply because he had some neck problems which made it impossible for him to write out a prescription without his hand shaking. He was losing confidence in himself and this was making him very depressed.

He had tried in every way to help himself and had even consulted many specialists but, by the time I saw him, he had almost given up hope of recovering and said he was on the brink of giving up his practice. This upset me because I knew that people like him were thin on the ground and that his patients would have been very sorry to lose him. Although extremely orthodox-minded, he was co-operative, and told me he would do almost anything to get rid of his problem. I advocated a change of lifestyle and suggested that instead of travelling between patients in his car, he should ride a bike. He laughed at this idea but was willing to take my advice. Manipulative treatment for his neck problem, as well as acupuncture, resulted in a dramatic change for the better and we laughed together about how he had cured himself by investing in a bike! He also discovered, as an extra bonus, a new pleasure to share with his wife, for she was keen to join him in his new hobby and together they enjoyed cycling in the countryside.

This shows that when a problem is tackled positively a wonderful change can come about, even in someone who has no desire to live any longer.

What is the purpose of life? This is a question heard often today, especially among the young. Life has a great purpose if we tackle our work and our responsibilities with love and devotion. Sometimes younger people, particularly students, find this difficult to accept: it is so easy to become depressed if we look at the state of the world and the many tremendous problems with which mankind is confronted.

This was brought home to me when tragedy struck a lovely family I knew in Holland. They had a most promising son. He was a potentially brilliant doctor but after an in-depth discussion one evening with a group of students on the many problems facing the world, he went home and turned on the gas-tap to bring his life to an end.

It was a devastating blow for his parents, yet they were not alone in their loss. There are many other comparable cases, all of them highlighting how dangerous it is to talk in negative terms about the purpose of each individual life. Although it is quite easy to lose sight of the meaning of life, happiness is within reach of us all. We must reach out and grasp it and if, sometimes, it appears to be elusive and beyond our grasp, we must keep on trying.

People who have suffered and conquered depression are very often the best people to help their fellow sufferers. This is why I am a great believer in the value of group therapy. Helping each other is the very purpose of our creation, as the early Christians knew only too well. They had been taught by Christ to "love their neighbours" and they understood that meeting with each other and sharing problems was something that God had intended for humanity.

This is a message which shines forth from the stories in the Bible. One of the most impressive tales from biblical days concerns the banishment of the Jewish people from Egypt. They had to work as slaves and could quite easily have been thrown into the very depths of depression. God, however, ordered that they should get together in their houses, and this meeting together and helping each other saved them from feelings of hoplessness and despair.

In the Acts of the Apostles we read how Peter was miraculously freed from prison and how his spirits rose when he knocked on the door of Mary, mother of John, and found that the Christians were gathered together praying for him. The very thought of being able to draw on the love and sympathy of good friends, coupled with a faith in a more glorious destiny for mankind, can do so much to lift the dark clouds of depression. Faith provides the encouragement to comfort each other, even in the darkest days, and when allied to prayer it can be a help in tackling many of the problems discussed in this book.

I recall a woman who was so frightened of almost everything that she became deeply depressed. Her doctor asked me to accompany him to see her one morning. I don't make house visits but in this case I decided to make an exception. We found the poor woman lying in bed drugged up to the eyeballs! Her doctor had done his best for her and she had also consulted a number of psychiatrists and private doctors without any sign of improvement. Then, just when her doctor was losing hope, he remembered that she had once asked him about alternative medicine, and so he contacted me.

He asked me what my initial thoughts were as I looked at her lying there. I gestured towards the bedside table which was covered with bottles of pills and said that I was surprised she hadn't exploded by now! It was a typical example of someone who had collected a new wonder pill from every one of a long line of doctors she had visited. Quite obviously she had indiscriminately lumped all her tablets together and had continued to swallow them night after night.

I asked permission to take her into my residential clinic to allow me to look deeper into the case. Her doctor agreed willingly to this request.

She was a difficult person to talk to, so I asked her to write down every dream she had and every thought she was willing to share with me. She agreed to do this and out of her dreams and thoughts I managed to fit the jigsaw puzzle together. In her life she had been through a great many different emotional experiences and had taken vast quantities of drugs which had affected her liver. Complexes and obsessions had started to rule her life and she was now questioning the reason for living. She continually asked me to be kind to her and I knew that with a lot of kindness she would confide in me. This she did, but I noticed that she never cried, either during or after talking about the past, not, at least, until the night when we were further into the treatment. She just couldn't stop crying and this brought her great relief.

In spite of her problems she had managed to hold on to her faith. She told me she prayed to God for help and, as she began to recover, I managed to interest her in some new activities which she greatly enjoyed.

She had quite a mixture of problems — depression with anxiety, frustration, resentment and agitation — and these problems had changed her personality. Her moods and attitudes were out of character, far removed from the person she really was. This often happens and consequently someone who is valuable and who could be of so much help to their families and to society, simply becomes a loss.

Another important factor which I managed to glean from her

dreams was grief. Where there is grief there are also very strong feelings, which must be dealt with. Once over this hurdle the woman was so much better.

Depression, which brings about depressive reactions, moods, experiences and temperament, is something distinct from depressive illness. Depression very often has a psychological cause and can become a predominantly physical problem. The manic depressive has totally lost any sense of reality and this is a problem which is very difficult to treat. In many cases it is a recurrent illness or melancholia, and it can be inherited.

Then there is a major problem facing many older people — senile depressions. These can usually be helped with treatment to restore the correct vitamin and mineral balance, as well as with some homoeopathic remedies.

Childbirth and the Change of Life can result in metabolic depression because they cause changes in a person's biochemistry and we often hear about post-natal depression or the "fourth day blues". It is quite normal for a hormonal imbalance to take place after childbirth. Nevertheless, I still advise great caution where diet is concerned.

Something else we hear a lot about nowadays is pre-menstrual tension. I often ask myself why so much is said about this and why it concerns so many women. I have found that a lot of pre-menstrual tension and menopausal depressions have their origins in the mind, in other words that they are psychosomatic. If, however, this is not the case, these problems are in need of specialised help.

During phases of physiological change a woman very often experiences a wide variety of autonomic and mental symptoms, and in many cases treatment aimed at the elements of autonomic function will do the trick without the need for hormonal regulation. In other words, it is possible to relieve the various disorders and symptoms, while at the same time avoiding hormone therapy.

The physical and mental symptoms most commonly reported are autonomic cardiac symptoms such as tachycardia, oppression, circulation problems, hot flushes, tinnitus, vascular headaches, gastro-intestinal symptoms, nervousness, depressive tendencies, anxiety, and disorders of sleep. I have found that the simple plant "Cimicifugae Racemosa" which is black snake root, is of terrific help to the autonomic and vascular nervous systems of women with these problems. Used in conjunction with Koemis Koetjing and Orthosiphonis, for fluid retention problems, it does a wonderful job.

With depressive reactions like anxiety it is difficult to concentrate. Depressive illness usually takes this lack of concentration a bit further and it becomes difficult for the sufferer to even think properly. In such cases marriages often break up under strain. I have seen many examples of this and I especially remember a case concerning a businessman in the entertainment world who consulted me. His depressive illness had driven away his wife. Then he received a terrific boost when, during the course of his work, he met another girl. She was, he said, much nicer than his wife and understood his condition very well. She gave him the support he desperately needed.

So why did he need help? He told me that jealous fears were creeping into his life and growing alongside his fondness for his new girl. Jealousy had been the root of his original depressive illness and now he was becoming quite obsessive about his new love. He fully trusted her but couldn't bear the idea of another man even looking at her.

Fortunately I helped him to overcome these fears by retraining his thoughts. I did this with relaxation treatment, a change of diet, vitamin and mineral therapy, and a simple extract of holly. His outlook altered amazingly and he is grateful that he can now live life to the full.

A high fat intake, cholesterol, too much sugar, a high protein diet, coffee, a high salt intake, emotional stress, alcohol, smoking, and a lack of exercise, are the ingredients in a recipe for disaster which has ruined the lives of many famous people.

Some of these factors had contributed to the downfall of one of Scotland's top football players who consulted me about a bad ankle. This great footballer, with whom I became very friendly, was in a very stressful situation. His ankle had been looked at by many specialists and he had been told he would never play football again. Naturally, he was bitterly disappointed that his talents looked like going to waste. The "final whistle", it seemed, had been blown on his career.

He then discovered that he had diabetes — as a result, I am sure, of the stress and depression he suffered after the traumatic news that he should hang up his football boots for good.

All wasn't lost though I treated his ankle successfully with acupuncture. His attitude changed almost overnight and before long he was back on the field as one of the most likeable and successful footballers in Scotland.

Many people have consulted me about various forms of depression. Some come in a really black mood. Some feel that they are in a dark tunnel with little hope of escape. With self-help and guidance, there is always light at the end of the tunnel. The sun can shine again, even for those who have lost sight of any ray of hope.

6

Hypertension

HYPERTENSION, or abnormally high blood pressure, is part of the price we have to pay for living in the fast lane.

In America, where life is probably more hectic than anywhere else in the world, the people know this only too well. The Americans, who are becoming increasingly health-conscious, are now as keen to know their blood pressure reading as they are to know their weight. I saw this for myself on a recent visit to the States. In nearly every chemist, or drug store, there were electronic sphygmomanometers which gave out instant blood pressure readings. After watching the reactions of customers who took advantage of the machine, I came to the conclusion that I don't entirely agree with this form of medical automation. While there are great benefits to be gained from people having regard for their own health by paying attention to diet for instance, I think there is a limit to any form of self-doctoring. In the drug stores I saw many people visibly shocked with the reading which registered on the dial. Perhaps their alarm was justified, although I am sure that most lay people do not understand the thresholds of blood pressure readings. They cannot, therefore, understand the significance of the figures which appear before them. Most people merely have a preconceived idea of what the reading should be, and if the figures do not correspond, panic sets in.

I am not trying to say that a careful check should not be kept on blood pressure. In fact, it should be watched very closely because, if ignored and allowed to creep up to a level where it is abnormally high, the results can be disastrous. I simply feel that a doctor or specialist is the best person to decide whether or not there is cause for concern. I have actually seen people going completely hysterical after taking their own blood pressure. This kind of behaviour quite obviously is enough to make anyone's blood pressure soar sky high!

The body's system which controls blood pressure can be compared to the central heating system of a house. If we look carefully at the heating system we see that it is the electric pump which forces water into the radiators. The main pipe leaving the pump leads into a number of smaller pipes and the pressure coming from the pump determines the amount of water sent on its journey through the house. The thickness of the pipes also controls the amount of water passing through. A change of pressure obviously allows more or less water to flow through the pipes. Corrosion or dirt are two factors which can bring about a change of pressure. In other words, the pressure dictates whether or not the system is in good working order and if the pipes, or the blood vessels, are clogged, the water or blood has less mobility. If this is the case, efficiency — whether from the heating system or from the human body — is greatly decreased.

Nowadays it is quite easy to measure heart and blood pressure. In doing this we get a clear indication of how healthy the blood circulation is, how well the heart is coping, and also of the effectiveness of the small arteries. Close checks should also be kept on the viscosity, or stickiness, of the blood. This is something which should not be underestimated because it clearly has a great influence on the entire circulatory system. Blood pressure lowers when nature causes the pressure to relax momentarily. This is why blood pressure is gauged on two levels — systolic and diastolic.

What is normal blood pressure? It is a difficult question to answer because there are many factors which have to be considered, including the temperament of the individual. Blood pressure is rarely consistent and can change by the minute. Nevertheless, the normal blood pressure for someone of about 21 years is between 105/62 and 140/88. Therefore, a younger person with a reading higher than 140/88 is quite likely to be heading for a lot of problems in later life.

How do we get hypertension and what do we do about it?

It is widely known that it can be the result of a kidney disorder. The British doctor, Richard Bright, said in his writings that patients with chronic nephritis often had an enlarged heart. Most sufferers of hypertension, however, don't have kidney problems. Most have bad dietary habits. Diet, and certain foods in particular, have a terrific influence on hypertension.

My wise old grandmother told me once that after a distressing spell with her children her blood pressure rocketed and she had to call in the doctor. He didn't prescribe any drugs but told her to drastically reduce her weight, cut down kitchen salt to a minimum, and take a course of castor oil. This was very good advice because we are now aware of how constipation can affect blood pressure, hence the reason why, in the USA, there are so many clinics offering colonic irrigation for hypertension sufferers. My grandmother followed her doctor's advice to the letter and has since passed it on to many others who suffered similarly.

Kitchen salt very often affects the pulse rate and the racing pulses of those who have a high intake of salt is often obvious to all practitioners. Salt, therefore, can be very dangerous and is one of the worst enemies a person with high blood pressure can have. Yet I am always amazed at the way such people, or even people with serious kidney problems, just cannot keep off salt. The very same thing is often found with migraine sufferers who know that chocolate is bad for them, but who are still tempted to eat it.

A woman who consulted me a while ago had quite high blood pressure and two diseased kidneys. She was addicted to salt and couldn't bear the taste of unsalted food. So in order not to be caught out, she carried a salt pot in her bag at all times. This kind of patient needs to be taught self-control otherwise they cannot be helped. They must also be persuaded to avoid kitchen salt. If they insist on something, a little Herbamare salt is best. Sufferers of very high blood pressure must stay away from salt at all costs. A heavy salt intake actually encourages high blood pressure and can also result in fluid retention.

I saw for myself in China something which Dr Vogel had been telling me for years — the importance of brown rice in regulating blood pressure. In fact, this wonder food is more important than anything else in the control of blood pressure. It has the best possible balance of yin and yang — positive and negative — and in China, where brown rice is the staple diet, the incidence of high blood pressure is very low compared to Western countries. Brown rice restores the elasticity of the arteries and, for this reason alone, it is also the best friend our blood circulation system can have.

Brown rice must be cooked correctly. Try the following method and you can't go wrong. Put the desired quantity of rice into a casserole or Pyrex dish. Pour over boiling milk or, preferably, water. Have the oven ready at the highest temperature, pop the dish of rice in and leave for only 10 or 15 minutes. Switch off the oven and leave the rice inside for five to six hours. Cut up some vegetables — parsley, chicory, celery and cress, for example — and mix through the rice with a little garlic salt. When required heat through.

Brown rice helped a young joiner to sort himself out. The 28-year-old explained to me that the nature of his work required him to eat huge meals. Looking at the 18-stone heavyweight, I was not surprised to hear that he had already suffered two heart attacks. He had been sent to me by his GP who was, quite simply, fed up with him. I discovered that my patient had been prescribed quite a number of different drugs and when I asked him to outline his eating habits I nearly took a fit! Breakfast started with bacon and eggs, followed by up to ten fish-fingers. I stopped him there. I didn't need to know more because I already understood his position well. No wonder his doctor was fed-up. The conscientious joiner had no intention of reducing his food intake because of the belief that he had to eat a lot to be capable of hard physical labour — a mistake made by many.

I invited his wife to come and see me and asked her a very direct question. Did she want to keep her husband? I explained to the shocked woman that this wouldn't be possible for much longer if his life continued on its present course. I then had a heart to heart talk with the portly fellow and managed to persuade him to carry out two of my wishes. The first was to stick to the reasonable diet which I had drawn up for him, containing large quantities of brown rice. The second was to practise the following exercise.

Sit down. Tell yourself to relax. Close your eyes and take in a fast deep breath, as deep as possible. Now let the air out slowly either by groaning or singing like the Yogies do with sounds of "ooo" and "aaa". Try to count to 30 or 40 before all the air is out. Repeat this for about ten minutes once or twice a day for several weeks. It is a sure way of lowering blood pressure. Alternatively, this can be done magnetically by placing a small 300 to 600 gauss biomagnet with the green side towards the temples, for 10 to 15 minutes a few times a day.

Six weeks later the joiner was unrecognisable as the same man. Completely off his drugs, he is managing a full day's hard work without problems, and without excesses of food.

There is a school of thought that people with high blood pressure should not take much exercise. I believe that responsible exercise for such people can be highly beneficial. The breathing exercise just mentioned, for instance, is perfect, and encouraging a plentiful flow of oxygen to enter the body, simply by walking in the fresh air, can do only good. Only a silly person would battle against hard winds or attempt to climb a mountain if their blood pressure was anything but normal. There is plenty of time for these and other strenuous activities once the blood pressure has been regulated.

Blood pressure will increase for a variety of reasons, including tension, stress, oedema, high viscosity of blood, blood vessel narrowing, arteriosclerosis, and kidney problems. Hypertension, brought on by any of these reasons, can often be successfully treated with homoeopathy, phytotherapy, exercise, and modification of eating habits. As always, diet is a vital factor and an appropriate diet for hypertension should contain endless bowls of brown rice and an abundance of fresh leeks.

High blood pressure, it could be said, receives more than its fair share of attention. Much less is said about low blood pressure, known as hypotension. When a person regularly feels faint or dizzy, hypotension is usually the culprit. Ninety per cent of hypotension cases are the result of improper activity of the gonad glands — the organs which develop reproductive cells; in a woman, the ovaries, and in a man, the sex glands. The gonads always respond well to a changeover from poor to healthy eating habits and they benefit from Dr Vogel's Kelpasan, as well as the herbal remedy, Hyssop.

I once had an employee who was totally opposed to the use of drugs. She even shied away from homoeopathic remedies and was a great believer in diet alone as a curative means. When she came at first to the clinic, she told me she suffered from hypotension, but she was not long with us when she announced that this problem had vanished. What brought about this dramatic change for the better? Quite simply, the sea and the use of Vitamin E.

Other treatment for hypotension is similar to that which I recommend for hypertension, but obviously different exercises should be practised. Hara breathing exercises are especially good. Also highly recommended for this condition are invigorating dry brush massages.

The importance of food for people with either hypertension or hypotension should not be underestimated. For more years than I can remember Gaylord Hauser has been advocating a natural diet which is known to keep blood pressure stable. When I last lectured with him in Los Angeles two years ago, I was reminded that he is the perfect advert for his own advice. He calmly but skilfully lectured for over an hour to a massive crowd. Without doubt a man who practises what he preaches. His basic philosophy is simply that a good, well-balanced diet is essential for a healthy body and harmonious mind. I sometimes use the example of Gaylord Hauser when trying to explain to people that blood pressure problems are usually self-inflicted, as the following story illustrates.

A businessman consulted me during one of the most distressing periods of his life. Although he was running a successful business he was harbouring a host of problems and when burglars rifled through his work premises, it was the final straw. He turned to drink and consequently lost control of his business, not to mention his private life.

His diet was poor and this, combined with stress, resulted in a bad case of hypertension. I advised him to waste no time and go into a residential clinic where his diet could be taken care of, and where alcohol was strictly taboo. Luckily he agreed. A fortnight later I went to visit him. What a surprise I got. Suffice to say, he was a new man. I was reminded of the "I am" diagram as I looked at his body, his attitude, and his appearance which had totally changed since his blood pressure returned to normal. After leaving the clinic, feeling fitter than ever before, he gave up the original business but soon became involved in another lucrative enterprise which he found very fulfilling.

In this case, and in others, I was most encouraged to see how the mind and body can be given such a marvellous boost by a few basic changes of lifestyle.

7

Hysteria

HYSTERIA is another manifestation of tension, a condition of extreme emotional excitement which causes an involuntary reaction, like, for instance, an outburst of violent physical activity. This is seen in the hullabaloo on crowded football terracings where pent up emotions boosted by the hectic excitement of the occasion, sometimes bubble over into rowdyism.

On the other hand, though hysteria is normally associated in the public mind with scenes of violence or near violence, where all rational thinking has been allowed to fly out of the window, it can bring relief to an individual by giving vent to his or her feelings of tension. It can be therapeutic for football fans, enabling them to give harmless expression to frustrations built up in their dull everyday lives.

Still on a sporting theme, I learned a lot about hysteria from, believe it or not, a racehorse! It was quite a famous horse which had been normal and successful for most of its life. As it approached an older age it developed some hysteric tendencies. This, the owner thought, was due to jealously of another horse, and she was sure it would right itself in time. But that did not happen and the hysteric condition became so bad that a veterinary surgeon advised that, if there was no sign of improvement in the near future, it would be best to have the animal put down. Naturally, the owner who was very fond of her horse, wouldn't hear of this and when a friend suggested it could be suffering from a back problem — something which I have often treated in horses — she brought the distressed creature to me.

When I heard the story I said I felt the hysterical outbursts were coming from psychological sources and, therefore, wasn't at all surprised when I learned about the horse's apparent jealousy. I turned instantly to homoeopathy and gave the horse Foliculinum, which resulted in an almost miraculous improvement in its general well-being.

Next, I inquired about the daily diet of the horse. This may seem strange, but diet is of equal significance in the treatment of hysteria in both human beings and animals and this vital factor was discussed in depth with the owner. I quickly introduced plenty of oats to the horse's mealtimes, which gave it a much calmer disposition. Oats usually make horses high but, consumed as part of a good balanced diet, they have a calming effect. Once more I used Avena Sativa, which was of benefit, and, after treatment, the horse was able to run in a very important race. This restored its confidence.

When parents notice hysterical tendencies in their children, something which can cause tension and even unhappiness in a normally peaceful household, the first thing they should investigate is the intake of sugar. Most children eat far too many sweets and this habit should be strongly discouraged. This advice, if adhered to, gives the treatment of hysteria a head start and, where there are indications of a tendency toward hysteria, can prevent its onset. Generally speaking, "kicking" the sugar habit, has a positive effect on a person's entire well-being.

I remember a teenager who came to see one of my physiotherapists. As she waited her turn she felt hysteria welling up inside her and her mother asked if I could help. First, I gave her a little shot of the homoeopathic remedy Ignatia, which worked wonders in calming her down. Then, looking ahead to a possible recurrence of the hysteria, I stressed the importance of diet to her mother. On her next visit I didn't need to give her a shot of the Ignatia. She was composed and obviously feeling a lot better. Her eating habits, her mother assured me, had been radically changed.

There are two kinds of hysteria. The first I would describe as a personality type, the second a form of illness. If we think about it we will soon realise that we know, or have met, someone with a hysterical personality. Sometimes they can appear quite reserved but then, as if deciding to become the life and soul of the party, they give quite extraordinary displays of their feelings and emotions.

It amazes me how frequently hysterical tendencies just cannot be suppressed. Indeed, some people seem to enjoy making an exhibition of themselves by acting hysterically. They feel that it lends significance to their personality in some way.

This is the reason why we so often find that famous actors can use hysterical tendencies positively to aid their performance. Sometimes, we see young people in the field of music or modern arts giving better public performances because of their ability to let their emotions take over their actions.

Over the years I have seen many people use such inclinations to their very good advantage. Unfortunately, I have also seen other cases, like Hitler, who deliberately provoked hysterical outbursts among Germany's youth.

Nevertheless, manifestations of hysteria are not only seen on large public occasions. Normally they come to the surface in homely surroundings. For instance, I remember a young mother who brought her son to me saying that she just could not control him. The pampered boy suffered from something which is fairly common — he hated school. At the same time every morning, about half an hour before the school bell rang, he began to complain of feeling sick and unwell. He was clearly feigning an illness to escape the classroom and when his mother tried to force him to go to school he became quite hysterical — to such an extent that his mother invariably gave up the fight and let him have his way.

The boy had been examined by doctors and specialists but they couldn't provide the distraught mother with the answers she was so desperately seeking. Eventually a psychiatrist diagnosed the boy's condition as the type of hysteria which expresses itself in a form of illness. The psychiatrist was right. The boy wasn't physically ill. He had a problem which was tucked away inside his mind.

I treated him with the help of homoeopathy and acupuncture and soon he was normal again. He grew up to be a very pleasant young man who, from time to time, felt ashamed at the memory of his outbursts and the dramatic way in which he had upset his mother.

If steered in the right direction early on, a person with hysterical tendencies can easily be helped to overcome them. At whatever stage, if we understand the conflicts within the mind and soul of the hysterical personality, their acting, thinking and communicating can be greatly altered.

Sometimes hysteria can surface in an adult following a change of lifestyle. Promotion at work, for example, can lead to a fear of not being able to cope. In fact, the very first sign of hysterical tendencies can be an inability to face up to responsibilities which a change of situation presents, and the result is often an illness, which can be very misleading and quite serious.

I remember a woman of about 35-years-old who consulted me in one of my clinics in England. She sat down and, before saying anything, she started sobbing hysterically. I calmed her down, gave her a homoeopathic tablet, and asked her if she had such outbursts often. She replied that they were becoming more and more regular. She looked desperately unhappy and I noticed she had four cuts on her arm.

She was reluctant to talk about the cause of her unhappiness but eventually, after I had won her confidence, she told me her story.

She lived in a flat, up several flights of stairs, with six children and a drunken husband. She barely had enough money to feed her family and had tried a few times to end her life, resulting in the cuts in her arm. She was not the suicidal type but had been left with a tendency to become hysterical in certain situations because of a traumatic experience in her youth when her father had tried to interfere with her.

A most unfortunate young woman, she urgently needed help. After a while I managed to erase her feelings of fear towards her father and I then started re-training her thoughts. To everyone's relief she found a job and started to stand up for herself a bit more. This had a good influence on the husband who cut down his drinking and the entire family became much happier.

The woman's mind was unbalanced because of the experience in her young life. This in turn had affected the husband, who turned to drink. When he saw his wife showing some strength of character and independence, he responded to this positive outlook and the whole situation became brighter. It was an episode which could conceivably have ended in disaster but didn't, largely as a result of the woman's commonsense approach to the problem and her willingness to accept advice.

Hysteria also responds well to "Hara" breathing exercises and autogenic training. Even so, sound advice, medical treatment and the best help in the world, can often fail to achieve results. When this happens, suicide — the subject I will discuss in the next chapter — can be an ominous threat.

8

Suicide

SUICIDE, which is on the increase in this country and elsewhere in the world, can be the result of a spur-of-the-moment decision or a carefully planned act. In whatever circumstances, it is an unnecessary wastage of human life.

Everybody has times when he or she feels deeply distressed, but to commit suicide is never the answer. Help is at hand for those who have hit rock bottom. There are doctors, counsellors, and self-help groups, not forgetting the Samaritans who have done a tremendous amount of good work in this field.

Sadly, however, many people who have thoughts of suicide don't give themselves a chance to be helped. Withdrawn into a shell, they are blind to the outside world and the arms reaching out to them. This is why we all have a duty to our fellow men. We must try to be receptive to their needs and notice when something is wrong. We must embrace them more readily, for this simple gesture can work wonders.

A large number of suicide attempts fail. Often this is deliberate. It is still a sad reflection on society though, that these desperate cries for help are allowed to reach such a pitch.

Suicide can rear its ugly head for many reasons. It can stem from feelings of inadequacy, hopelessness, or loneliness. The man who is overburdened with problems and cannot carry the weight which has been placed on his shoulders, thinks of suicide as an escape route.

BY APPOINTMENT ONLY

For over 40 years now this growing problem has been very much on my mind and my heart always goes out to people who are feeling suicidal. Perhaps this is because, as a mere child, suicide made a great impression on me. I had a good friend who was a wholesale grocer. Sometimes, as we sat in his small warehouse between the bags of dried fruits, flour and sugar, he shared his feelings of loneliness with me. Many times, he a man and I a child, put our heads together and tried to solve the problems of the world. It was possibly an unusual relationship but I was the only person in his life with whom he could share his troubles.

One day, as I was on my way to school, I noticed a commotion outside my friend's premises with cars and people gathered around. Young as I was, I boldly marched right into the warehouse where I saw my old friend hanging by the neck beside all the sacks of flour we used to sit between. The impression that sight made on me I could hardly comprehend. Later in life, after experiencing a few more traumatic events, I always tried to put myself into the position of the person who was contemplating suicide. This, I am sure, has helped me to save many from this final act.

It is frightening to think that well over a thousand people in the world commit suicide every day. Every year well over half a million people take their own lives and even more attempt to do so. Suicide statistics fluctuate from country to country and it is interesting to look at the kind of people who feature most strongly in the figures. In Britain one in fifty doctors are said to commit suicide, while in the USA, gardeners are prominent in the statistics. In Holland the highest number of suicides are committed by farmers. Why do professional people, gardeners, farmers, or anyone at all for that matter, end their lives so tragically? The reasons are many, including a broken home, loss of self-control, drug or alcohol addiction, and depression.

It is easy to understand why doctors are prone to the thoughts of suicide. Every day they are faced with misery and suffering that can result in an inability to escape from work pressures. Any doctor can experience so much inner conflict that suicide seems to be the only escape route.

I was once asked to help a farmer who was tied up in knots

because of an exaggerated concern for his livestock and harvest. There were a few problems and the farmer thought that everything in his life was going wrong. He couldn't sleep at night and his thoughts were constantly filled with despair. By the time I saw him he was feeling very suicidal and it was quite a job to help release him from his chains. Gardeners often turn to suicide because of loneliness at work. Working alone, they can easily become introverted and find it difficult to communicate with their fellow men.

People who suffer from hypertension and take certain drugs to control blood-pressure often have suicidal tendencies. Different kinds of drugs have been known to spark off negative emotions. Not long ago a certain sleeping tablet had to be taken off the market because a number of people who were taking it as part of long-term treatment became suicidal.

Proof of the link between drugs and suicidal tendencies was clearly indicated in an industrial town in England in the 1960s. In one year 460-480 people tried to commit suicide. The following year this figure doubled. The dramatic increase became the subject of investigation by an independent group of people. Did it relate to the industrial environment in which people were living? What about financial problems, alcoholism, drug addiction, sexual problems, or was it anything to do with long-term drug treatments?

The research group worked closely with local doctors who agreed to identify the people who were taking drugs for insomnia. A significantly high use of sleeping tablets was revealed. The researchers talked to people taking these tablets on a long-term basis and, with the help of the doctors, the tablets were phased out. This resulted in a speedy drop in the suicide rate.

Nevertheless, the feelings which drive people to commit suicide usually stem from conflicts between the mind and body. Our diagram reminds us that the soul affects the spirit and our actions, and where there is conflict, there is normally also lack of communication. This conflict must be tackled before the welling up of suicidal feelings can be curbed.

I remember a woman who asked me for help after she had taken an overdose. Very suicidal because of loneliness and a complete loss of her powers of communication, she had withdrawn entirely from life. She was once a well-known musician but no longer did the sound of music fill her house. After talking to her I searched through my mind for a story to inject value into her life, and I discovered one which gave her renewed strength.

It was the tale of an old violin, which I heard shortly after I arrived in Scotland. The violin was in an auction room waiting for a new owner but bidding had barely got off the ground. Anyone could have bought the idle instrument for a few pennies. Then a man asked if he could play the violin. The sound of strings filled the hall and when the beautiful music ended, bidding began in earnest. The hammer fell and the violin was sold for an unbelievable sum.

I explained to the woman that although she thought she was of no use any more, her life was still potentially very useful. The purpose which was missing had to be regained. I managed to put her in touch with people and, although she too was old like the violin, she began again to use her great gifts. Her dignity returned and she became of tremendous help to people who were going through traumas similar to her own because she understood exactly how they were feeling. As this story highlights, those who have been on very high hills and landed in very low valleys, can be of the greatest help in our community.

If we are tuned in to the right wavelength there is balance and purpose to life and this is the most wonderful situation. One of the best ways to tune in to life is to start the day with a song. This gives us sunny feelings and is a super tonic for one of our smallest glands — the thymus — which most people consider to be one of the least important glands.

Looking at our glandular system, we see that the Pituitary Gland performs a number of vital functions. The hypophysis is the conductor of the endocrine glands and controls the thyroid and adrenal glands. It is a direct link to the controlling nervous system and especially to the hypothalamus. We know that all these organs work like a musical instrument. Like a piano, therefore, they must be kept well-tuned in order to be capable of giving a good performance.

Pay attention to nutrition, sleep, exercise requirements, and breathing, and these glands will perform well. It is often said in medical books that the thymus gland is of very little importance and that the older we get the more it shrinks. Medicine today is beginning to take a second look at this little gland and it is now accepted that strengthening of the thymus can have the same effect on a person's emotional status. The thymus also has a very close relationship with the reproductive organs and is weakened by envy, suspicion, and fear, and strengthened by love, faith, trust and courage. Strengthen the thymus gland and the Life Force within us is given the most marvellous boost.

As said in the first chapter, the Life Force, or energy, is vital, but it can only be increased or sustained if the body, mind and soul are cared for. The Life Force is influenced for good or for bad by the arousal of positive or negative emotions. Television violence, or a disturbing story in a magazine, for example, can sap our energy and weaken the Life Force.

I very often state that we are living in a low-energy, thymus-weakening society because this gland is constantly attacked both physically and spiritually. Some people also believe that the day we are born influences the ability of our thymus to cope with this blood-spattered environment.

A young person came to see me who, admittedly, had good reason to be at breaking point. After talking to her I advised her to change her lifestyle. I told her about our musical gland system and recommended that she treat it much more carefully in the future. She received acupuncture and colourtherapy and it pleased me very much to see what an interest she took in them. I showed her the diagram and explained how many secrets hidden in the eye can be revealed through iridology. This interested her so much that she began to study it and it brought a whole new meaning to her life.

Another case which I found very encouraging concerns a man who wrote to me from prison where he was serving a life sentence. Although I did not, in any way, condone the crime he had committed, I was sympathetic when I discovered he had cancer. This was his reason for writing to me; he was seeking practical advice because he wanted to do everything possible to help his diseased body. Every time I received a letter from this man I asked myself what in the world has he got to live for when

there is only a prison wall in front of him. Before too long I got
the answer. He worked so positively to overcome his cancer that
the medical profession welcomed his findings on the disease.
Therefore, in spite of two major drawbacks — having cancer and
being imprisoned — this man worked to make his life of value to
others.

In one of the letters I sent him I said that we are all born with
the seeds of degeneration and that it is our responsibility to
regenerate ourselves. To be able to do this, I said, we must
influence our mind and body positively.

Another case of a patient who had taken an overdose comes to
mind. This very pleasant man was ashamed of his actions but,
nevertheless, told me he would do it again given the chance,
because his life was totally meaningless. Until a short time
before, his life had been very productive, but because of
disappointment he had aged greatly and cut himself off from
society. He asked me what I could do with such an old, dried-out
prune which was almost lifeless.

The previous day I had visited one of my former clinics,
Mokoia, where I had been reminded of life's little miracles, and I
started telling him about my journey into the past. As I talked I
noticed a flicker of interest in his eyes.

In the back garden of the old residential clinic were three
beautiful big trees. The sight of them transported me back to
Holland and the time Professor Geers, a good friend, had
presented me with a tiny box. He told me it contained seeds
which he had acquired in Canada. He said he had never before
seen such magnificent pine trees and, because he knew I was a
nature lover, had elected me as the one to attempt to grow them
in Holland. I was very busy at the time and although delighted
with his gift, put them away in a drawer and accidently forgot all
about them. Four years later they were found and I decided to
take the precious box to Scotland with me.

Once there, I gave them to my gardener and asked him to plant
them, but he too put the seeds in a drawer. Another three years
passed until the gardener drew my attention to them, pointing
out that they were as hard as stones. He remarked that the bin
was the best place for them. I refused to throw them out and told
him that nature has the most amazing powers, that they should

be given the chance of life. I was thrilled when more than half of the 12 seeds sprouted and some years later the trees stood nearly as high as the house.

I concluded this story by telling my patient that he also had not turned to stone and persuaded him to think positively and to recognise that there was life in him yet. Today, this man is once more industrious and happy. Every time he begins to feel like an old dried-out prune again he remembers the three majestic pines. It does wonders for his self-esteem.

There are surely comparable stories, as well as help, for everyone who feels suicidal — stories which could stimulate positive energy and create bright hope instead of dark despair. Meanwhile, it is a sad commentary on present-day society that so many people are driven to take their own lives in a last desperate bid to draw attention to their plight.

9

Psychosomatic Problems

THE CLOSE relationship between the mind and the body is generally recognised. The blush on a person's face as a sign of embarrassment or the palpitating heart after a fright are two simple, everday examples of their inter-connection. The mind can, however, affect the body in much more harmful ways leading to what are known as psychosomatic illnesses — illnesses which are most difficult to diagnose because there are no apparent reasons for their occurrence.

The mind is prone to retain its secrets, particularly when they are hidden away in the dark, inner recesses of the subconscious and this is, in fact, the crux of what is a two-way problem. On the one hand, a positive, optimistic outlook and a pleasant sunny disposition, which is often the result of a happy childhood, can be invaluable in promoting physical health. On the other hand, a negative, pessimistic outlook can lead to all kinds of bodily problems.

In the past the idea that serious physical ailments could have their origins in the mind was frequently dismissed. Now, in more enlightened times, the idea is more readily accepted. The mind affects the body, but the body also affects the mind: aches and pains can be clues to mental disturbances which, if they are left to smoulder, can have serious consequences for the entire personality. Every psychotherapist will confirm that such mental disturbances are not only detrimental to the body, but can result in a person becoming entirely lost to reality. Fortunately, psychosomatic problems are now being taken much more seriously and are being carefully studied.

The word "psychosomatic" was first used in the 19th century by Johann Heinroth, the German missionary. It means "body" and "soul" and I feel sure that even so long ago he must have known of the link between spirit and physical illness.

The solution to these types of illnesses can often be found in the sufferer giving vent to his or her feelings. The trouble starts when our emotions are pent up. Unexpressed hope or fear can result in a nervous stomach or vegetative nerve problems. Fortunately, these conditions can be helped with some wonderful herbal remedies like Hypericum Gentiana and many others.

In order to keep our body and spirit in balance we must keep a careful check on all our emotions. The complexities of the human brain are quite amazing. It is a marvellous storehouse of memories, good and bad. Everything that we have ever experienced in our lives is filed away in the subconscious, only requiring the right association to be triggered back into our awareness. The trouble starts when a patient is lacking this association and unpleasant memories remain buried in the mind as the source of psychosomatic illnesses. The cure, of course, is to unearth the memory and bring it to light, often displaying to the conscious mind that it was originally of little consequence. This, however, can be a very difficult and lengthy process.

I recall a woman who was brought to me because she couldn't walk. Many doctors had examined her, but could find nothing wrong. I worked night after night on her case and eventually the cause of her trouble was identified. It was of a psychological nature and after placebo treatment her health improved overnight. She has been walking tall ever since.

Many people use a certain incident in their lives as an excuse to feel ill. Often they feign sickness to draw attention to themselves and win the comfort and sympathy of friends, as the psychiatrist and psychotherapist know only too well. The proof of this is shown in the number of people who visit me on a Monday morning after reading the doctor's column in the *Sunday Post*.

I remember a very intelligent woman who was convinced she had multiple sclerosis after reading an article about it in the paper's weekly medical report. She compared her symptoms with those of an older woman whose case was highlighted in the report and found that they corresponded exactly. She told me that these symptoms had appeared about a year ago. She was in her late forties and when I told her that multiple sclerosis was diagnosed in the majority of cases before the age of 40, a look of utter relief showed on her face. That was the last I heard of her multiple sclerosis.

How many people, I wonder, cling to these beliefs and use them as an excuse for imbalance between their mind and body? King Solomon was indeed wise when he advised his people to "keep their hearts with all diligence for out of the heart flow the issues of life".

Heart problems, or a broken relationship leading to what we call a "broken heart" frequently result in psychosomatic problems. As a young boy, I once asked if our hearts had anything to do with our minds. I was told that the heart was in the mind. I don't know if I entirely agree with this, but I do know that there is a definite link between the heart and the mind. I have made a careful study of heart transplants and read that a patient who had undergone a transplant operation was asked if he felt he had changed emotionally. He replied that his attitude had changed greatly.

Many doctors have criticised me because I can't accept that the heart is simply an anatomical or mechanical organ. In homoeopathy it is vital to recognise the link between the heart and the mind and I don't know if any homoeopathic practitioners could think otherwise.

Some years ago I went over to The Hague with Professor Roger MacDougall to give a public lecture. Afterwards I was approached by a woman I had first met many years ago in my clinic in Holland. Fifteen years had passed since we last saw each other, but she had not changed at all. She was riddled with psychosomatic problems and had never allowed herself to be helped.

On this occasion she seemed delighted to see me but I could not refrain from being slightly rude to her as, before I got the chance to ask how she was keeping, she blurted out that she was no better. With more than a hint of annoyance in my voice I told her that her attitude was just the same as it had been fifteen years before. I thought back to those days. On every visit to the clinic she started complaining to my colleagues the second she entered, saying how dreadful she felt. I often admired the patience they had with her. So as she stood before me fifteen years on, I told her that I didn't think she would ever get better and went on to have a long talk with her.

That evening her husband telephoned our hotel to speak to me. He congratulated me and explained that whatever treatment I had given his wife, had worked marvellously.

Sometimes psychosomatic problems, which have been building up for years and are deeply seated need just such a good shake-up. This was how an old doctor I once knew cured a wealthy woman who said she couldn't leave her bed. Doctors and specialists had carried out all possible tests on her, tried every reflex, and couldn't find anything wrong. The old doctor asked me to act as a witness one day. I was to stand in the corner of the room while he attempted a new approach in treating her. We entered the room where she lay miserably in bed, obviously feeling sorry for herself. He walked over to the bed while I moved towards the corner of the room. He talked sympathetically to her and asked if she ever felt lonely. Then, to my surprise, he started to take off his jacket, then his shirt, then his shoes! Next, still talking sympathetically, he began to remove his trousers as he told the woman that he was going to jump into bed beside her to keep her company for a while. At this, the woman shot out of bed, ran like an athlete towards the hallway and shouted for help. The doctor's treatment, though a trifle unorthodox, had been highly successful!

Very often patients suffering from psychosomatic illnesses need proof to back up what the doctor tells them. I remember a patient who was convinced he had a tumour in his cervical vertebrae and who simply refused to believe any doctor who told him that this was not the case. Eventually, I arranged for an X-ray to be taken. This provided the proof that there was no tumour and when he saw it for himself he was a happy man.

One of my patients, whom I dearly cared for, had

psychosomatic problems. She also needed some kind of proof. Basically a nervous person, she had a number of obsessions and every time she saw me she had a different story to tell. They seemed so real that it was difficult not to believe them. Sometimes they were tales of the past, sometimes of the present. Once she was convinced she had been the cause of an accident. Another time she imagined she had pulled the emergency brake of a train and caused great harm. She also believed that she had pushed someone from the pavement into the path of a car. The stories were getting more incredible every time and although everyone, including myself, went to great lenghts to persuade her that they were all in her imagination, she couldn't accept this and had to endure terrible distress and sleepless nights.

This certainly didn't help her general nervous condition. On one occasion she told me a story which was so far-fetched it was a little frightening. I just couldn't convince her that it wasn't true. Fortunately, at that time, Hans Moolenburgh, who is a first-class psychologist, was staying with me. I asked if he would be kind enough to see this patient because I felt I could help her no more. So far many doctors and psychiatrists had failed, but, because I liked her so much, I could not bear to throw in the towel as well.

My friend agreed to see her and after doing so offered a simple solution. He asked me to do a very strange thing. I was to pick up my prescription pad and put down in black and white that she had never done any of these things she had imagined. I had to state that I would take responsibility for saying this and I signed my name at the bottom.

It worked. As soon as I gave the piece of paper to her and told her to keep it carefully, her attitude brightened and she quite obviously escaped from the mental chains which were restricting her from leading a normal life. When I saw her a few years later she was still enjoying freedom from her self-made prison and still had the little piece of paper which had changed her life.

Whatever the causes or symptoms of psychosomatic illnesses, the entire working of the mind, body and spirit, and their inter-relationships, must be taken into consideration before help can be given. The problem is often deep-rooted, requiring long sessions of psycho-analysis. On the other hand, sometimes all that is needed is a sensible explanation, giving the patient the strength and the will to recover.

10

Alcoholism

"GOOD HEALTH!" is an expression often heard among friends before strong drink is consumed in the highly-charged atmosphere of a public house. But no two words have ever been more misplaced. "Here's to your bad health!" would be a much more appropriate salutation. The notion that drink is good for you is no more than a sales slogan thought up by advertisers. Drink can undermine health and, when taken in excess, can lead to what is becoming a monstrous problem in our present-day affluent society — Alcoholism.

People who are compulsive drinkers to the extent of becoming alcoholics have their moments of artificially concocted happiness, but these are short-lived. More often as slaves to the bottle — no longer masters of themselves — they exist in the very depths of misery and despair.

It is a very complex subject, alcoholism, and there is often an intricate personality network which has to be investigated before the reasons why a person drinks too much, or is an alcoholic, come to light.

I was made very aware of this when, after lecturing in London a short while ago, I was asked to speak to a young girl who had become an alcoholic. Her eyes shone with hope as she talked to me about her problem. It was the kind of look I see often in the faces of people who desperately want to escape from the hazy world of alcohol.

I learned from this girl how easy it is to become dependent on alcohol. At a young age, her well-meaning parents actually encouraged her to drink by offering wine at the table. She didn't like it but because she wanted to act "grown-up", at the tender age of 14, she persisted and eventually began to enjoy it. As she approached 16 and was experiencing all the normal ups and downs of the middle teens, concerning school work and boy friends, she started to drink a little more. So when a boyfriend took her to a pub she was no longer new to the drinking game and found she could "down" a fairly liberal dose of the "hard stuff".

A broken love affair drove her to more drink and when problems arose at home she turned to the bottle for consolation. Soon she lost control of her drinking habits and became an alcoholic. This addiction made it almost impossible for her to continue with her studies. She was trapped, and in a further bid to opt out of her responsibilities, turned to drugs. The situation was fast becoming disastrous. Her young life and happiness were clearly at stake and, although she managed to give up drugs just in time, nothing seemed to be able to drag her away from alcohol. She almost begged me to help her. Naturally, I said I would and I am pleased to say that the treatment I gave her — I used acupuncture in conjunction with a high dosage of Vitamin C and yeast as well as an anti-alcohol tablet — worked wonderfully.

People are brainwashed by seductive advertising and conditioned by a long-standing convention which links the ability to take a "good drink" with sophistication. Generally, habitual drinkers have no real idea of the risks they are running. Alcohol and drugs influence the functioning of the brain to the extent that several brain centres are blocked and cannot operate normally. Others can operate but not at full power. These are medically-established facts. It is also known that the continuing use of alcohol and drugs can result in paresis, incomplete paralysis, and complete paralysis, because of the toxic effects they have on the body.

I remember a man who was caught up in a terrible situation. He had been an alcoholic for 27 years and only came to see me after much persuasion from his wife and friends. I had a long talk with him and I soon realised that, in regard to his state of health, he was rapidly approaching a crisis. In other words, for him the pub closing time call of "Time, gentlemen" was threatening to take on a more sinister meaning.

He had run out of money — a frequent problem with those who must spend their money on drink — but I decided to help him free of charge because he was obviously so desperate and willing to co-operate. He showed many signs of improvement after acupuncture and some remedies, including one specifically to help the brain. In addition, I gave him Loranthus, mistletoe from the wild oak, which did a wonderful job for his absentmindedness. Life started to flow back into him. His eyes lost their glaze and when I met him three years later he told me he had found a whole new lease of life and had regained the respect of his family.

I was shocked, therefore, when five years later I met him again sitting in my waiting room and looking at me helplessly like a naughty schoolboy who had been caught stealing from the cake-stand. He explained rather sheepishly that his son had come home from abroad waving a bottle of liquor and that, without thinking, because it was New Year, he had accepted a small measure. Unbelievably, that very afternoon the lure of the pub was irresistible and in a couple of hours he undid years of progress towards better health.

The moral of the story is inescapable. It shouts from the rooftops the awful truth — once an alcoholic, always an alcoholic. Not even the tiniest sip of the poison is permissible.

I had to be honest with him. I told him that, out of all the alcoholics I had treated over the years, only a few had refused to co-operate and that they had come to a very sorry end. Some had committed suicide and others had ended up in the gutter or had gone to prison. He nodded his head sadly and told me that it was this knowledge which had made him return to seek my help. He had no wish to return to the life of hell which he had lived for 27 years.

It is widely known that alcohol changes the personality, especially when drinking is excessive. I have seen the finest people becoming completely different, in fact, almost unacceptable, as a result of their drinking. I have heard them making excuses for their tendency to imbibe, excuses which emerge at first as "white lies" but which are soon transformed into downright dishonest deceptions. Their downfall then rapidly gathers pace and quite often even the most intelligent and respectable people develop tendencies towards crime.

All this should be a warning that alcohol must be treated with great caution. The all-important Life Force can start to suffer as soon as drink is consumed on a regular basis. Another effect of alcohol on the body is a bunching together of the red corpuscles in the blood which reduces the flow of oxygen and immobilises certain enzymes.

A hangover and a pounding heart are common symptoms experienced on waking up after a night of drinking. They are only part of a long list of horrible experiences which are induced by alcohol. Besides, to go back to the theme of diet and health, alcohol destroys valuable nutrients in the body and it could therefore be said that "you are what you drink"!

An attractive woman, who was clearly suffering from an over-indulgence in alcohol, came into my consulting room. She told me that she had to drink for stimulation. Otherwise, she said, she felt dead. She reminisced about her eventful past and explained that it was only with the prop of alcohol that she could look at her present life and see any real purpose. I pointed out to her that it was utterly wrong to think of alcohol as a stimulant and explained that all it did was to pull the brakes on the part of the brain which controls our attitudes. I told her bluntly that she looked like a victim of alcohol. It was a remark intended to strike home, and it did. She started to question the value of life, opening up at least a little chink of daylight on a road which was clearly leading her into a pit of despair.

I then took her outside and showed her a beautiful dwarf crocus and asked her if she or the crocus had the greater Life Force. The question seemed to puzzle her and she laughed. I illustrated the point I was trying to make by drawing her attention to a cluster of little crocuses which had pushed their way up through a thick layer of tarmac. I explained that they had once grown freely with ample nourishment from the rich soil in a little border round my front door, but that because of the need for more parking space the area had been covered with the thickest possible tarmac. Nevertheless, despite their imprisonment, the little flowers had so much Life Force that they had been able to push through the tarmac to bloom again.

This simple story taught her a lesson. She appeared to be deeply touched and afterwards expressed a new willingness to fight the addiction which had controlled her life for years and which had caused damage to her liver. Cirrhosis of the liver, incidentally, is known as the "drinker's disease" — with ample justification. In the chapter on depression, listing the enemies of the liver, I had no hesitation in putting drink at the top of the danger list.

Alcohol isn't only a threat to our bodily health. It is one of the biggest factors in the build-up of carnage on the roads. An Australian report showed that one in every two road accidents had an alcohol factor. One in every five hospital admissions was linked to excessive drinking. Two in every five divorces were caused by alcohol, as were three out of every four criminal assaults. The list of social misbehaviour and tragedies resulting from an over-dependence on the bottle is endless.

Not all alcohol problems end in tragedy. In my experience, I have seen many happy endings in cases where drink was clearly driving people to disaster. Just recently I saw a very happy man. Eight years ago I helped him to stop drinking. He had been a very heavy drinker and because of this his marriage was on the rocks and his business in a slump. Only when he had agreed to consult me had his wife given him a final chance.

I took him into my residential clinic for intensive treatment. In the first place he needed rest and understanding. Secondly, I gave him autogenic training as well as several natural remedies. It worked and today he is at the helm of one of the best businesses in Scotland.

Another leading businessman, who came to me some years ago, had gambled away a million pounds because of alcohol. The addiction made him careless. Every time he received a tax form or bill he couldn't be bothered to deal with, he threw it into a rapidly rising heap of unattended documents. He too could have been rescued, but sadly he was too late when he came to see me looking for help. His heart and liver were in such a bad state that there was no hope of his recovery and, shortly after, he died.

I once read about a little boy who was asked for the definition of a promise. He said: "A promise is I must, I must, I must — until I do it." Too often, I find people who are addicted to alcohol are prepared to say "I must" over and over again, but then forget all about it. People can usually tell when drink is reaching the stage of taking over their lives and this, surely, is the time for them to seek help before it is too late. There are many people who can help, including the Alcoholics Anonymous Association. Group therapy or a practitioner who is prepared to listen, can also give invaluable assistance, the more so if the victim is genuinely anxious to help him or herself.

One of my patients saved up the money he would have spent on drink in a year. It was such a sizeable sum that he was able to take his wife on a world cruise on board the *Canberra*. That's what I call positive action.

Why does a person become dependent on alcohol? It can be stress and strain of modern life, depression, unhappiness, marriage problems and so on. There are plenty of reasons why people want to opt out. Indeed, the way in which countless thousands are looking for an artificial means to find release from stress reminds me of the flight of the lemmings. Usually people are in search of the simple joy of being alive or the wonderful feeling of childhood.

I have before me what almost amounts to a book written by a young, attractive woman, whose life became meaningless simply because in her teenage life, and in her married life, she couldn't stop thinking back to her joyful childhood. Her marriage broke down and she turned to drink, all the while subconsciously thinking of the happy, carefree days when she was a child, living blissfully in the protective care of her mother. This was a typical case of the mother-child relationship which we often meet in women as well as in men and, because it is so often divorced from reality in a person's later, mature years, can be a source of all kinds of emotional and psychological problems.

Sometimes it is said that alcohol is a stimulant for the thalamus, but as I have already pointed out, alcohol is never a stimulant. Not so long ago a wealthy woman came to see me. She was a typical example of someone with too much time and too much money. She told me she was dependent on the stimulation of alcohol and when I explained that alcohol was not a stimulant, but something which could do untold harm, she strongly contradicted me. I could see clearly that she was going to pay no attention whatsoever to my message and that she would just have to learn the hard way. This she did and about a year later she returned to me with a sheepish look on her face. She admitted I had been right and promised me her full co-operation. This time I was able to help her.

Some cases of alcohol abuse, however, are so far advanced that there seems to be little hope of recovery, although I have seen very bad cases respond to remedies like acupuncture, yeast, Vitamin C, and anti-alcohol capsules. There are many other remedies which can help a person to break the habit of drinking day in and day out, but one of the most vital aids to recovery is a large helping of understanding.

The greatest help of all is the realisation by the alcoholic of the tremendous damage he is inflicting upon himself. One way which I encourage this realisation is by showing an alcoholic a Kirlian photograph taken after he has consumed a stiff drink. The aura of the brain is quite clearly broken up and when I take another photograph after no alcohol has been consumed for several weeks, there is a smooth aura, very different from the previous one. This visual proof of self-inflicted damage invariably gives the alcoholic a big jolt which encourages cooperation.

I worry about women who drink during a period of pre-menstrual tension or the change of life, because alcohol can cause lipotozemia as well as hormonal disturbances resulting in a lowering of oxygen in the tissue cells and the impairment of the immune system. This is defined in the excellent book on the subject, *The Health Revolution* by Ross Horne, who gave me a copy when I met him in America. He said this particular practice could lead to such a break in the immune system that there could be a greater risk of cancer.

Cancer — the very word conjures up fear in the minds of millions. It can, however, be avoided to a great extent by healthy eating and healthy living, as well as by general recognition that alongside alcohol at the top of the cancer danger list are a high fat intake, too much sugar, smoking, lack of exercise and too much salt.

I personally know how right Ross Horne is in regarding the lowering of oxygen in the tissue cells as a great danger because I studied this particular subject with Professor Asai of Japan, who has had great success in his research on oxygen.

Alcoholism is a universal problem but it is much more prevalent in some countries than in others. In Scotland, for instance, hospital admissions for male alcoholics are seven times higher than in the rest of the United Kingdom and five times higher for women. Men and women of every age, even teenagers and younger children, consult me because of an alcohol problem. It is such a pity to see them, devoid as they are of the incentive to live life to the full.

On the other hand, it is most encouraging to see how the Life Force can be restored with the right help and how people who have been cured of alcoholism can be of greatest help to others.

There is life after drink. It is wrong to believe that a person who never touches alcohol is some kind of social outcast. In my own experience, I have ordered non-alcoholic drinks on numerous occasions, even when privileged to be in the company of the famous and royalty, without the slightest remark being passed. I am never ashamed to order a soft drink, because I know only too well what misery and traumas anything stronger can bring.

11

Allergies

ALLERGIES have recently surfaced as something worth more than merely a passing interest. Quite dramatic symptoms have been traced to them and a great deal of time and effort is now being spent on this problem.

I became very aware of this two years ago while on the platform alongside a medical professor. We were in Toronto and about to lecture to a large audience. I learned the professor's interest in alternative medicine had been kindled after a family upset concerning allergies. He told the Canadian audience a most interesting story about his daughter, and consequently his enlightenment.

His daughter was a very promising student who, towards the end of her studies, had started to experience traumatic changes in attitude and personality. The professor had tried to identify the reason for these changes but to no avail. At that point he enlisted the help of several colleagues. Still there was no luck: the girl's personality problem remained a mystery. As a last resort the girl took tranquillisers which were prescribed for her by a psychiatrist. Following this step she just got worse and worse.

Her father was by now very upset and growing desperate as he watched the deterioration of his daughter. He then heard about a naturopath who, although without medical qualifications, had successfully treated many people. The professor decided to try him. To do this he had to summon up a fair amount of humility but, as we all know, this is easier when the health of a loved one is at stake. He accompanied his daughter to see the alternative practitioner who astounded my friend by announcing that the girl had a food allergy. The naturopath went on to outline his proposed treatment for the girl and the professor had no hesitation in saying he would co-operate fully. The girl's response to the treatment was incredible. Immediately her physical and mental health picked up and within a few months she was her old self again.

Her father was so impressed that he started to study alternative medicine and has now become quite an authority in various areas of this field. I feel a great affinity with him because I understand the joy which such enlightenment can bring for I too, unexpectedly, turned the very same corner.

What exactly is an allergy? It is a reaction between an allergine and an atopic reagent. The allergine is the external substance which provokes a reaction in the body — the atopic reagent. These reactions can be acute or slow. For instance, the person who has an allergy to pollen will experience a quick reaction. Other allergies take much longer to produce symptoms which convey to the sufferer that something is wrong. These slow reactions are often much more dangerous.

A simple way to describe an allergy is to say that a person has a high sensitivity to something — possibly plants, foods, fabrics, floor polishes, medicines or paints. The most innocuous things can cause allergies. Who would think that fresh fruit or the harmless primula plant, for example, could give untold misery to a human being? Foods like fish, fats and animal proteins are common causes of allergies, as are wheat and some other grains. Some people also discover they are susceptible to allergic reactions as a result of house dust and mites, or even cats and dogs.

What can we do about these allergies? First of all we must find out exactly what the allergy is and then treat it by counteraction such as immunisation by antibodies. The Nogiers method used in acupuncture, which I use from time to time, aids the discovery of hundreds of allergies. Using this method I have found that even the slightest trace of perfume is capable of causing an allergy.

A surprising enemy which we never think twice about, is milk. We are becoming a nation of "milkaholics" gulping down at least a pint of milk a day. I can assure you that there are more problems caused by drinking too much milk, or by drinking milk at all, than people realise. One young mother who came to see me was allergic to milk and I advised her on what to drink instead. She didn't take my advice and became addicted to fizzy cola. Before long she was back before me complaining that her hair was falling out and she was feeling dreadful. It took me quite a while to convince her that she had to eat a healthy diet in which fizzy cola and other unacceptable foods were banned. This time she took my advice and changed into a healthy mother whose baby was equally healthy.

Many babies are not so fortunate. A surprising number of them are allergic to their first food — cow's milk. Don't let us forget that cow's milk contains twice the amount of protein as human milk and the poor baby just cannot cope with this high protein intake. This common allergy among babies results in swelling to their faces, especially the lips. It looks as if the little baby has been poisoned and if not properly dealt with, cow's milk can indeed act like a poison.

It is easy to shrug off this allergy and think that the baby or child will outgrow it. This may appear to be the case but it is almost weekly that I treat children with asthma or eczema who were taken from their mother's breast and given powdered or tinned cow's milk instead. It can be that an asthmatic child is quickly relieved by an antihistamine, but this is far from being a cure and something more has to be done. The psychological aspect of asthma has to be considered and this can often be helped with homoeopathy. The possibility of an allergy to milk should be considered. Also possible is a deficiency of lactose, an enzyme which helps to break down milk in the bowels. If this is the case, a milk-free diet is the answer.

Another seemingly innocent everyday food, which is frequently the cause of allergies, is an egg. People react to this with amazement and , looking at me in disbelief, say: "What in the world can be wrong with an egg?" If they only knew how many people I have helped simply by asking them to stop eating eggs!

One of my patients who was very set in her ways, had this allergy. She had feelings of nausea, headaches and sometimes felt dizzy. I asked her to remove eggs from her diet and to substitute them with artichokes when they were available, and if not, to use boldocynara which is an artichoke extract. The next time I saw her she was a changed person. She told me that if I had put her on a strict diet she could not have coped. It was necessary for her to gradually change her lifestyle. This she was able to accept and the gradual process boosted her Life Force which made her feel healthier than ever before.

Yet another food which can be a rogue is wheat. I once carried out some research with Roger MacDougall, who advocates a gluten-free diet for the control of multiple sclerosis. We had long discussions on gluten, which is the protein in wheat flour, and on the very common allergy to it.

Wheat is one of the finest products given to man but, ironically, man's interference has turned it into an enemy for many people. Wheat in its natural state should contain four chromosomes per cell but, according to research carried out a few years ago, this figure is now nearing the forty mark.

This sad tale of the deterioration of wheat reminds me of the book by Gunther Schwab, *The Dance with the Devil*, which shows how much destruction man has been responsible for and how artificial manuring is killing the finest of wheat, one of nature's greatest gifts. It is wrong to believe that we will get used to inferior wheat or other produce. We must understand that consumption of these things can lead to allergies which in turn can lead to unpleasant problems.

I remember a child who was suffering because of an allergy to a certain foodstuff. The mother approached me in Bienne, Switzerland, some years ago when I was lecturing with Dr Vogel. She asked us to take a look at the child, saying that he was in a dreadful condition. As we were only on a visit, we didn't have the material to find out what food the child was allergic to. However, after looking at the symptoms — dizziness, skin problems and bad breath — we decided to treat the liver. Dr Vogel prescribed a high dosage of Kelp, as well as some Echinaforce. This treatment did the trick and the child's condition quickly returned to normal and stayed normal, as was related in letters from the mother in which she thanked us most heartily.

Another allergy case comes to mind. The patient was behaving like a drug addict and, after carrying out a Kinesiology test, which is specific muscle testing, I discovered that she was allergic to coffee. I then learned that her daily intake of coffee amounted to at least ten cups. The woman could hardly believe it when I explained the cause of her trouble. I told her that one cup of coffee contains approximately 130 milligrams of caffeine. Multiply that by ten and, whichever way you look at it, you have an assault to the system. I told her to stop drinking coffee and, on doing so, to expect headaches which were, in fact, withdrawal symptoms. As soon as the headaches diminished she felt fine and remained so as long as she steered well clear of the coffee bean. In fact, she can't even stand the smell of coffee now!

Asthmatic people, as well as being nervous individuals, are usually allergic to something. One man I helped was very asthmatic but not long after I treated him, he was back in my consulting room complaining that his asthma was as bad as ever. After a little investigation I discovered that the recurrence had been sparked off because he was using synthetic paint to brighten up his house.

In a similar case, a patient's progress was reversed as soon as he started working with chemical pesticides. I recommended to this patient, a book — The Silent Spring by Rachel Carson — which warns of the modern-day dangers regarding pesticides and would make anyone step cautiously in future.

I have talked a lot about the reactions which an allergy provokes. What about the more common allergic reactions? These include a running nose, wheezing, itchiness, excessive gas, diarrhoea and constipation.

Is it possible to be allergic to a smell? I can personally vouch that it is because I have experienced it myself. I love the city of Edinburgh but not when the dried-peas' smell of the breweries engulfs it, for this immediately gives me the most thumping headache. Again, on my visits to the Far East, smells have triggered off headaches. This was exactly what happened the last time I paid a quick visit to India.

One woman who consulted me was very depressed and almost suicidal. After a lot of investigation I discovered that she was allergic to the smells of the chemical factory near her home. There was only one answer — she had to move house, and having done so, returned to normal health within a few weeks.

As already said, people can be allergic to the most unlikely things. When I practised in Birmingham I came across a great many immigrants who were all experiencing similar unpleasant problems including headaches, diarrhoea and colitis. Eventually I found out that these people were allergic to the city's drinking water and as soon as they changed over to spring or mineral water, their problems disappeared. We also know that one to five per cent of the population are allergic to water which has fluoride added to it.

Coping with food allergies can be tackled in a variety of different ways. Discovery of allergies is not quite so easy. Trial and error is the way most people tackle the problems but the adoption of the Rotary Diversified Diet makes it easy to pinpoint food allergies. This diet is given quite clearly in the book *Allergies* by Dr Theron G Randolph and Dr Ralph W Moss.

Allergies often disappear as soon as the sufferer adopts an organic or wholesome diet. A diet packed with additives and synthetic ingredients is certain to predispose allergies. For a patient I saw not long ago, who suffered from bad asthma, I advised a drastic change of diet — as well as Echinaforce, certain herbs, and a regular dose of Vitamin B12. This advice was taken and the asthma disappeared.

I am often asked why I don't advocate the greater use of vitamins. I believe that if the diet is balanced, there is no need for extra vitamins. Unfortunately, however, the diet of most people today is not well balanced and requires to be supplemented with vitamins and minerals.

There are certainly key deficiencies in the body at birth. Sometimes these deficiences are God-given tools to find out where we have to change our direction. These tools must therefore be used to chip out a new lifestyle, incorporating a proper diet. This alone will change a person's outlook and make them so much healthier and happier.

In days gone by skin or cloth tests were used to try and

discover allergies. Today there are easier ways like blood or hair tests, but the best method of all is kinesiology which is specific muscle testing.

There are those who believe that too much time is spent on the problem of allergies. I disagree with them. It is no coincidence that in these days of increasing environmental pollution, more and more people are discovering they are allergic to something or other. This problem is only the tip of a monumental iceberg.

12

Diet

THERE IS a growing interest among people in what they can do, not only to ward off illness, but to enjoy positive good health. This is reflected in the questions which always come fast and furious at the end of my lectures.

On these occasions, over the years, I have tackled many thousands of questions, but I especially remember one put to me by a woman. It was simple and pertinent. She wanted to know what I regarded as the most important treatment in medicine. I didn't have to think long before answering, because as every good naturopath knows, among the many facets of alternative medicine lies the key factor in all nature cures — diet.

Acting on this truth, a naturopath will always pay attention to the basic laws of nature. He will look at the body and, bearing in mind the "I am" diagram, will carefully note the physical appearance which can provide vital clues as to how well or how badly a particular body is cared for.

Hippocrates was right when he said: "Your food must be your medicine — and your medicine your food", and in reflecting on the truth of this statement, I am greatly indebted to Dr Alfred Vogel, who, for over sixty years, has been preaching that diet is the basis of good health. He in turn was a pupil of Dr Max Bircher-Benner, Dr William Schwabe, and Dr Madaus. In my practice over the past 25 years, I have become increasingly convinced of the correctness of their view that a balanced diet is the secret of good health.

I could easily write a whole book on the value of diet based on my experiences. I have worked in this particular field for so long that I can tell merely by looking at the physical appearance of a person what, if any, health problems he or she has, while at the same time reaching a conclusion of what is good or bad for that particular individual. However, as this book is intended to help those with nerve and stress problems, I will concentrate my advice in that particular direction. In doing so, the question immediately arises — what has diet to do with the brain? Or, to be more exact, what has diet to do with our nervous system?

Many moons ago a patient handed me a book written by Dr George Watson, entitled *Nutrition and the Mind*. I read it with great interest and returned it, forgetting to take a note of the publisher so that I could obtain my own copy. The lender has now left the country and I have searched everywhere for the book, but in vain. The book was especially interesting because it related how the author's wife had gone through a sudden personality change. On one occasion she was sitting quietly reading a book when she jumped up, stormed out of the door, and threw herself in front of a car. Luckily she was rushed to hospital in time and survived.

Naturally, the husband was greatly relieved but he didn't leave the matter there. He searched for the causes of the sudden change in his wife's outlook and discovered that the high protein slimming diet which she had adopted had affected her mind to the extent that she became suicidal. Consequently the doctor made a close study of his wife's eating habits and the change of diet he advocated helped her mind to stabilise. As an added bonus, she reached her ideal weight with very little effort.

I once lectured to a group of medical students who had requested a talk on acupuncture. It was to last the entire day and when I spent nearly the whole of the morning session talking about diet they were obviously displeased. One of them reminded me of their original request and I placated him by saying that I would talk about acupuncture for the duration of the afternoon. Meanwhile, I wanted to make sure they all knew as much as possible about the highly-important subject of diet. I was too well aware that medical students and doctors have a knowledge of first and second-class proteins and carbohydrates, but know very little about a natural balanced diet. It is vitally important that they should be acquainted with the diet nature intended for us because, regardless of treatment, good health just cannot be built on the foundation of a poor diet.

One summer, my old gardener showed me two strawberry patches which he had cultivated. In one he had used artificial manure to feed the plants, but in the other he adopted more old-fashioned methods using organic manure. The second bed produced strawberries which were much superior to those "reared" on artificial food. Not only was their smell much nicer, their taste was unbelievably different.

Human beings, when it comes to diet, are not so very different in their needs from these strawberry patches. Our well-being depends on how we feed ourselves. If we want to look, taste, smell and feel good, we must eat the right food.

This is quite clearly illustrated in the "I am" diagram. Take a look at the skin, hair, nails and general lifestyle of the person next to you. It is just a matter of looking. The evidence of a poor diet will be unmistakable.

I remember reading a very interesting article in the *Reader's Digest* on how much diet can influence the nervous system. The article, headed "Your Meals Can Affect Your Brain", contained some startling new scientific evidence about the food we eat and how the brain responds to nutrients. Much of this research is focused on neurotransmitters, the chemicals through which the brain's neurons, or nerve cells, communicate with one another.

The brain is protected from many substances which can be in the bloodstream — for example, harmful chemicals or helpful drugs — by what is known as the "blood-brain barrier". Only a few chemicals can pass through this barrier. Food is broken down into individual nutrients which enter the bloodstream. They can then travel through the brain where some can affect the brain's neurons and encourage the production of neuro-transmitters. This means that the brain is undoubtedly affected by what we eat.

In newspapers and magazines recently we have read a lot about the amino acid, Tryptophan, which can induce sleepiness and because of this has been the subject of considerable controversy. It acts as a catalyst in the production of Serotonin, the neurotransmitter which makes you sleepy. In other words, the brain neurons need Tryptophan to produce Serotonin. So how do we get Tryptophan into our brain? There is very little of this amino acid in protein, but research has revealed that eating carbohydrates gives Tryptophan a much better chance of crossing the blood-brain barrier.

A good naturopath always recommends a diet containing plenty of unrefined carbohydrates. Vogel, for instance, has said that carbohydrates are important fuel for the nervous system. He also believes, as I do, that protein intake should be kept low. Carbohydrates increase the body's secretion of insulin, which clears the blood of other amino acids as they flow into the muscle cells, giving Tryptophan a better chance to enter the brain. The ideal diet to achieve this is one which is well-balanced and that is something of particular importance in cases of severe depression which is thought to be relieved by Tyrosine, another amino acid.

In the same article the part which Lecithin can play in helping the memory was discussed. This is of special importance to old people who, in their later years, tend to become more and more forgetful. Here again, however, to achieve any success, Lecithin should be given in combination with a balanced diet. Indeed, the moral of the article was that people with nerve problems can help themselves by eating foods supplemented with nutrients which feed neurotransmitters.

This field of research is vast and these are still early days. Nevertheless, it offers great promise and in these modern times, when nervous tension is becoming more prevalent, it will be followed with growing interest.

Science and technology are playing an increasing part, not only in the prevention of disease, but in the promotion of good health. This was brought home to me at a meeting I had with Dr William Kelley of the United States, who is head of America's Council of Nutritional Research. Dr Kelley, whose work emphasises the importance of diet, has perfected to a fine art the use of a computer to discover allergies and health problems in his patients. I was highly impressed by the results he achieved with sufferers of schizophrenia; and also by the work carried out by the Brain Bio Centre in the States, on nutritional counselling.

Meanwhile, it is shocking to learn that in America, almost a third of the people are either physically or mentally sick, with mental disease at the top of the list of all illnesses. In Britain too we have our full share of people who are mentally sick. In a census conducted as long ago as 1964, it was shown that British industry was losing eighteen million man hours every year through psychiatric illness.

How do we combat such shocking statistics? We simply cannot afford to have so many people continuing to feel sick or below par. There is clearly a reason for their sickness. There is a cause for every symptom of illness which must be dealt with.

In looking for that cause, as well as what we have already discussed in this book, the building up of a healthy mental attitude, equally deserving of our attention is a regard for the words — "You are what you eat". The basic rule to remember is to select foods which are as natural as possible. The next rule is to balance our food. It was never in God's plan to feed us with poisonous preservatives or dangerous coloured foods. Chemically-produced foods cause a lot of harm and much of their nutritional value has been destroyed. Why, I often ask myself, can't people leave things alone? Why do we have to interfere so much with nature? We have even interfered with a simple thing like our drinking water and this is shocking and quite unacceptable. It can even be harmful, causing sickness and disease. The use of pure drinking water, free from additives, can be of great benefit as a substitute for food during a regular cleansing period for the body. In other words, fasting if carried out properly can do no harm, although it is sometimes advisable to seek expert advice before launching on a period without solid food.

I have always been amazed to see how crystal-clear patients in my residential clinic have become after a short period of fasting. It shows what a marvellous treatment it is for the brain. Even a very depressed and nervous person can reap great benefit, and if the fast is followed by a good balanced diet, some exercise and plenty of oxygen, his misery can be replaced by an entirely new outlook and a new zest for living.

We must conquer worry and try to maintain a tranquil mind and a positive attitude. We must stick to a balanced diet of natural foods. We must drink pure water, fast now and again, ensure that we take plenty of exercise, expose ourselves to sunshine, and take enough rest and sleep. This is a code of practice which, if followed faithfully, will be a worthwhile investment in good health, often showing results beyond all belief.

Food is a gift from God which should be loved and respected. It is sad to see how little respect it gets today. I once visited a family at dinner-time and ended up feeling very sorry for the mother. Eight people were sitting around the table, each eating a different dish which the mother had prepared in order to satisfy their whims, likes and dislikes. The meal looked like a free-for-all with all the participants bickering and not even tasting, never mind chewing their food properly.

It was a scene which helped me to understand why there are so many people with constipation and indigestion problems. Chewing food is very important. Saliva has an important job to do and we must help it. It is the fluid secreted in the mouth to soften foods and aid digestion. To enable it to do this efficiently, we must masticate food properly before it enters the digestive tract. If this was done more a lot of hiatus hernia could be avoided.

As an onlooker at this chaotic meal-time, which was not unlike "a chimpanzees' picnic", I was reminded of an old biblical saying — "Better is a dinner of herbs, where love is, than a stalled ox and hatred therewith". This in turn reminded me of a lecture I heard given by one of the top French nutritionists, Madame La Blanc. She observed that a plant eats minerals, an animal eats plants and man eats animals. "Who eats man?" she asked. "If we can't feed each other or be of help to others, or not even show love and respect what is the purpose of life?" she added. Her philosophy of life was that if there is no love and respect for each other there is no purpose in living and I agree with her view.

On the question of diet again, after talking to patients about what foods they should avoid they invariably ask if there is anything left for them to eat. This question is, of course, a product of conventional thinking. When I tell them about the abundance and variety of foods which can be part of a healthy, balanced diet they are often incredulous. Their eyes widen with surprise when I mention the natural foods which are so much more nutritious and tasty than processed rubbish.

Rice, for instance, is the best yin and yang food. It is widely used in the Far East, where I have always been impressed by the fantastic variety of delicious brown rice dishes. It isn't always appreciated that rice, as well as being tasty and satisfying, is a wonderful health remedy. I always tell students that they will never make good acupuncturists unless they believe in a good yin and yang diet.

In Holland and in this country I have always been surprised by the number of people consulting me with vegetative dystonie, one of the many disorders of the nervous system which are psychological. Vegetative dystonie is a complex ailment encompassing the following symptoms, which cannot be attributed to any organic disease: vascular spasms, sudden sweating, cramps in the vascular system, internal problems and organic neurosis — all of which can be greatly helped with a good balanced diet and herbal remedies.

Gastric ulcers, cirrhosis and eczema also respond well to a natural diet. The lack of bowel bacteria, which makes people lethargic and devoid of energy and nervous, can be successfully tackled with a high intake of natural yoghurt. In addition, a natural diet should always contain some raw vegetables and fruits, although we often advise that they should not be taken together.

Dietary requirements vary so much that the best diet for a person is one which is tailor-made to suit him. I am often asked what my own basic diet is and I frequently notice how surprised people are at how little I eat. Years ago Dr Vogel suggested a diet to me which I still regard as a very good general diet for people with nerve problems:

Breakfast: Muesli mixed with the juice of an orange, grated apple, half a banana or other fruit. One or two pieces of ryvita or wholemeal bread spread with natural vegetable margarine (sunflower or corn oil). One cup of tea after the meal, preferably peppermint, rose-hip or camomile. "Bambu" coffee may be used as an alternative.

Midday Meal: One plate of fresh vegetables, especially of carrots and beetroot. Some other raw and cooked vegetables. The fresh vegetables can be mixed with a little sauce made from olive or sunflower oil with a little lemon juice or celery juice/sauce. Baked or steamed potatoes in their jackets may be taken with the vegetables. For dessert take yoghurt (low fat) with honey.

Evening Meal: Muesli, then fresh fruit salad. If you have a tendency to indigestion do not eat those together. Vegetable soup from vegetable remains, made with apple, radish, figs, leeks and tomatoes, flavoured with Kelpamare. Use salt sparingly, a little Herbamare salt is much better.

General: Animal fat is prohibited. Use eggs sparingly. No white flour, white sugar (or products made with them), pork, sausages, bacon or ham. Cut down, or even better omit completely, coffee, alcohol, nicotine and sweets. Take enough outdoor exercise in order to obtain fresh air. Increased activity is recommended. For example, walking instead of driving or being driven.

The body is a unique, highly-intricate machine, which we can destroy by eating the wrong food. I cannot stress enough how important it is that we eat good food. This was brought home to me one day when, having some free time, I went to the supermarket with my wife. I had often wondered about the expense such a visit entailed and that day I saw for myself where the money was going. I could hardly believe my eyes when I saw the vast array of junk food with which I was confronted. There were all kinds of sugary puddings, tins of tomato soup which had never seen a tomato, and numerous other products which, although attractively wrapped, were virtually lacking in anything which could truthfully be described as nourishment.

The check-out answered my question concerning the money. The woman in front of us had two enormous trolleys full of groceries, yet her bill came to only half the price of my wife's small box. I saw the reason when I looked at the woman's provisions. It was all cheap junk food. This provided all the evidence I needed to substantiate what I had already guessed — that she weighed at least sixteen stones!

Foods should be carefully selected. This isn't difficult. There are no mathematics involved in calculating what is good and what is bad, just instinct. We all have this instinct but too often it has been smothered by conventional thinking, slick advertising and old wives' tales. We have a natural power of selection, enabling us to choose between foods that are beneficial and foods that are useless, but sometimes this instinct needs to be aroused.

We should never hesitate to ask questions about exactly what we are buying. Questions are so often worthwhile and stimulating, as I have found at the end of my lectures, which is "Question Time". I always enjoy those sessions and often marvel at what I learn from the questions and the exchange of experiences that is never in short supply.

Once, when I was lecturing in Canada, I asked a member of the audience who had posed a question, to stay behind. I could see that he had been an extremely ill man and my assessment was shown to be right when he told me that he owed his life to a macrobiotic diet which he had adopted when his cancer had reached an advanced stage. I was interested to hear that his initial reaction to this radical change of diet was an improvement in his nervous system. In fact, my interest was so strong that I went to one of the finest teachers of macrobiotics in the world and asked him to teach me as much as possible about the diet. I have since advised a number of people to adopt a macrobiotic diet and I am happy to say that in all cases it achieved positive results.

Alexis Carrel, a Nobel prize-winner, said that the doctors of today must become the dieticians of tomorrow. How true. We must not close our minds to the subject of diet. There is so much to learn and so many myths and misconceptions to wipe out — for instance, the animal protein myth. Contrary to popular claims, animal protein is a poor source of energy, whereas a good complex carbohydrate diet is rich in energy-giving properties. Vegetable proteins such as soya, vegetables, and nuts, are first-class and do much more for the body than all the animal protein in the world!

Similarly, we must not forget that most "whole" foods contain their own natural salts which are so much better than ordinary kitchen salt — a product which should be carefully used, or substituted by sea salt or Herbamare salt. A high intake of fats should also be avoided. A great many products, harmless-looking and familiar on millions of dining tables, are a threat to good health. Indeed they have become so much a part of the established pattern of eating that people are prone to jump to their defence.

A woman once asked me after a lecture what I had against sugar and demanded proof of my claims about it being an enemy of health. I told her there was no need for me to give her proof. All she had to do, I said, was write to the British Dental Association and ask for the statistics on the number of people in Britain with healthy teeth. I told her to expect that not even two per cent of the British population had what could be described as healthy teeth. What better proof could there possibly be than the sorry tale told by such figures? In sharp contrast, in countries which we call "uncivilised", I have seen people using their big, white teeth like pliers. They eat sugar but only in the form of cane sugar, barbados sugar or honey, and not the white rubbish which is consumed in such huge quantities in the Western world.

Another deadly enemy is white flour. The enormous use of it in this country is appalling. It was once rich in nutrients, but now most of them are bleached out of it. We are all living creatures and we need living food. White flour, which forms the basis of so many of our loaves and cakes, is lifeless.

Now, unfortunately, many of our wrong eating habits are being exported for purely commerical reasons, to Africa, Asia and elsewhere. I became acutely aware of this after a wonderful lecture by Professor Ayotella of the World Health Organisation in the Middle East which I was lucky enough to attend. The theme of his talk was the aim of the WHO — to achieve health for all by the year 2000. This is something we are all yearning for and working towards, but following the lecture, when we were sitting together in a corner, I told him I was doubtful about his dream being fulfilled on target. For as we were speaking, between mouthfuls of the delicious health-giving milk of the King Coconut, scores of little dark children were coming in clutching the rubbish which we have exported to them, cola drinks and chocolate bars.

I am convinced that this kind of food will never help us to reach our goal. Time after time I have seen healthy people in other parts of the world suffer because of the processed foods which we have given them. Did the Creator of man not provide us with sufficient natural foods? Do we really need to process and damage food in the way we are doing? The answers to these questions shine out from foods which no one has tampered with and which are crammed full of electro-magnetic energy. The value of this energy for health is underlined in a book by Dr Hazel Parcells, which contains the most wonderful recipes and which she was good enough to send me. What she preaches in the book will open the eyes of every kitchen chemist. She stresses the importance of achieving an acid-alkaline balance in our diets, believing that this contributes to a sense of well-being. Foods with high quantities of electro-magnetic energy strengthen the body's defence mechanism and, coupled with an acid-alkaline balance, can rid people of many of the causes of nerves and bad health generally.

In addition to a good diet, nerve problems can also be helped greatly by a simple manipulation of the spine. High intakes of fat and cholesterol are often the cause of hypertension and coronary arterial disease, both massive killers which react well to manipulation together with a prescribed low protein diet with no fats, a restricted salt intake and an avoidance of gas-forming foods.

People who are specially prone to suffering from stress should be careful about the quality, quantity and digestibility of the food they eat. Stress is frequently the result of a lack of understanding of the body's digestive system and metabolism and important factors in a low stress diet are how we are eating and what we are eating. The golden rule is to eat small meals and only when we are hungry — simple rules which, if they are adhered to, can minimise stress and neutralise harmful emotions.

To a great extent, it is a question of self-discipline and self-effort, which reminds me of what one of my great teachers, Dr Allan, often said in his lectures — "We have to play a great part. God will work with you but not for you."

One day, after leaving my surgery, I passed a café and noticed a mother coming out with a child on her arm. In one hand she had a bag of chips and in the other a packet of aspirin. I was sorry to see this, because I knew that the one follows the other and both are unnecessary. This story again illustrates that we are what we eat and so does a story I once heard about a small village in South Africa.

A mother had left her little baby in the back garden to bask in the sunshine for a few minutes. When the mother returned there was no sign of her baby. There was still no sign after an intensive search. It was a complete mystery. Years later, a few people were looking from a distance at a group of gorillas passing by. One of them was acting strangely, slightly differently from the others. The villagers went closer for a better look, saw that the creature looked almost human and decided to try and catch it. This wasn't too difficult and it was soon in a cage awaiting a visit from the village doctor who declared that it was a human being. The villagers were dumbfounded and questioned the doctor's judgement, but eventually it dawned on them that this was the long-lost baby.

It took a long spell of different feeding and re-educating of manners to bring this gorilla-like individual back to being a normal human being. This was eventually accomplished, proving that we really are what we eat!

A lot of unhappiness, rooted in psycho-physical illnesses, can be avoided if natural foods are eaten. Diet is no more than commonsense. It is a false conception that people who follow the laws of nature are cranks or fads. The cornerstone of all natural healing is summarised in the statement: "All healing comes from within and the body heals itself". It is essential to realise that every disease has its positive aspects. Disease indicates that our immune system is being weakened and tells us that there is an imbalance in our bodies, leading to the discovery of negative energies. In time, perhaps after a little treatment, the healing process will naturally restore balance.

A bad diet always results in sickness. A sedentary lifestyle, which incorporates an unhealthy diet, unnecessary stress and so on, provides a breeding ground for disease. It is our responsibility to be diet-conscious although the medical world must also shoulder some of the burden of educating the public in healthy eating habits. As Thomas A Edison said so well: "The doctor of the future will give no medicine, but will interest his patients in the care of the human frame, in diet, and in the cause and prevention of disease."

13

Anorexia Nervosa

OPEN ANY magazine and what do you see? Slim-figured girls, slimming articles, and special diet foods.

Diet and health today receive mountains of publicity and although I believe this is quite right, it does tend to encourage stereotyping of the body. In other words, the "ideal" body is everywhere you look and everyone wants to be slender and sylph-like. Many women especially feel pressurised by this image and in desperation to attain the "right" kind of body, blow up diet matters out of all proportion. Taking diet out of all perspective, they walk head first into a lot of problems, one of which is extreme emaciation, such as is found in cases of Anorexia Nervosa.

Anorexia Nervosa, which journalists call "the slimmers' disease", is usually suffered by girls in their late teens and early 20's but it can affect any age group, as well as both sexes. It is a self-inflicted disease, caused by a distorted body image and a belief that certain foods and in some cases, all foods, are harmful because they will make the body grow fat. It is a problem which doesn't appear overnight and this is why the sooner it is diagnosed the easier it is to treat. Treatment is important because, untreated, Anorexia Nervosa, can be fatal.

Many people suffering from this disease enjoy the feeling of being empty. There is no doubt about it, an empty stomach stimulates the brain, but a constant feeling of hunger over-stimulates it to the point of disorientation.

It always shocks me to see young enthusiastic people become so anxious about their dietary intake that they lose all commonsense. Sometimes when I see them it is too late for me to help. I'm glad to say, however, that in most cases of this kind which I have dealt with, I have been able to help, especially when the psychological side to the illness is not too fully developed.

I remember one girl who ended up in hospital. Her weight had dropped from well over 10 stones to under six stones and she was just a poor little creature. She made little headway with psychiatric treatment and eventually had to be fed intravenously. Her trouble started when she became over-concerned about eating certain foods which she quickly decided to omit altogether from her daily diet. She then became obsessive about food in general and found hardly anything to be acceptable. Before long she was showing obvious signs of being undernourished and her body had shrunk to skin and bone. Her father urged his daughter's psychiatrist to grant permission for her to see me. This given, I was able to start her on acupuncture treatment to which she responded very well. I also gave her the wonderful herbal remedies from Dr Vogel — Centaurium and Neuroforce. After three weeks on this treatment she improved greatly and felt a lot happier within herself. She even managed to sit her exams which, to my delight, she passed in spite of having missed a lot of work because of her stay in hospital.

The story of this girl should be a lesson to anyone who is about to embark on a slimming diet. In fact, it is very dangerous to go on any kind of strict diet without first consulting a doctor, dietician or naturopath. Often they are the best people to advise on a diet which is truly balanced. Before this can be possible there are always adjustments to be made. It is not realistic suddenly to omit certain foods — meat for example — from the diet without looking at mineral and vitamin intake. These are vitally important and great care to prevent deficiences of them must be taken.

Another diet-related disease, not so well-known as Anorexia Nervosa, but sometimes close on its heels, is Bulimia Nervosa, a nervous disorder which results in a morbid hunger. Until fairly recently little was known about this malady because the sufferers didn't advertise their condition. Most look as if no problem exists. They are usually not underweight and it is interesting to note that many enter into the disease quite innocently. After having over-indulged with food, the sufferer then proceeds to make himself or herself vomit. This works quite well, at least as far as maintaining a stable weight is concerned, but the vomiting is habit-forming and the patient begins to actually enjoy the experience. This leads to an inability to stop forcing himself or herself to bring up all he or she eats.

It is interesting to note that in ancient Rome this was an approved practice. Great feasts were held, sometimes lasting several weeks, and during this period the guests were plied with food continuously. A room called the *vomitarium* was set aside where the guests could rid themselves of what they had already eaten so that there was room for more food.

People indulging in this habit can often be recognised by the huskiness of their voices. Continuous vomiting tends to take its toll on the vocal chords.

I remember a very nice young farmer's wife who got into this habit. She consulted me after she had been on a slimming diet for a number of weeks. Unfortunately, she had taken the diet to the extreme and was making herself sick after every meal. This practice resulted in Bulimia Nervosa and it took me a long time to retrain her mind and rid her of her obsession.

I have also treated a considerable number of people who went on to different diets, became obsessed with cutting down food intake, and made themselves desperately ill.

Pressure is often put on young beautiful girls who are slightly overweight. They are constantly told how charming they are but that, in order to become "perfect" they should lose a little weight. Again, this can result in their becoming obsessive about attaining the ideal body to the extent that commonsense is thrown to the wind. They select a diet, any diet — it doesn't matter to them whether or not it is sensible — and change their eating habits overnight. Such conditions are a perfect breeding ground for nervosas and before long these girls can find themselves fighting a long and weary battle for health. In many cases they are not capable of fighting single-handed and need the help of a doctor or specialist.

I remember one girl who was like a walking skeleton with no beauty left. Yet all she saw when she looked in the mirror was fat! People suffering from Anorexia Nervosa often pendulum between obesity and malnutrition.

One of the great dangers after diagnosis of Anorexia Nervosa, is a subsequent vegetative nerve problem. I have seen some people, now completely normal, who did not receive the necessary treatment for the vegetative nerve system. As a result the situation grew blacker day by day. However, as soon as the vegetative nerve system was properly treated they made a dramatic improvement.

The dangers of obsessive dietary approaches are beyond comprehension. This is clearly illustrated in a case I dealt with involving a young man who became so mentally ill through diet that he nearly committed suicide. I helped this poor fellow by giving him the Vogel remedies already mentioned in conjunction with a daily injection of Coliacron, a brain enzyme which I discovered in Holland years ago as the most marvellous way of helping Anorexia Nervosa, anxieties, phobias, psychological complaints. stress symptoms, neuro-vegetative dystonia, disturbances of the cerebral metabolism, and retarded development — both mental and somatic.

All of these problems can be greatly helped with a well-planned programme of treatment, but many could have been nipped in the bud if the right communication had been established at the right time.

14

Deficiencies

THERE ARE numerous health problems which have been caused by deficiencies and, in relation to nervous disorders, I would like to mention some of my experiences in dealing with them. It comes immediately to mind, that a number of years ago, a lady came to me who was diagnosed as being manic-depressive. She was in quite a bad state and had gone through the normal channels of different treatments, had seen several psychiatrists, and consulted her doctor regularly. With several drugs the symptoms had been slightly alleviated, but she was a very unhappy woman. Just by coincidence, after having treated her, I gave her a multivitamin, because I thought she looked a little off colour. This vitamin had to be taken along with the remedies from her own doctor. Within a fortnight her improvement was so miraculous that I did not think this was entirely due to the treatment I had given her. My treatment was only a relaxing exercise but, to maintain the progress, I kept her on this multivitamin. The improvement was quite surprising and, after a month, she said that she was sure this was due to the tablets I had given her. I carried out another research on the tablets but could not find anything other than that they were quite high in the "B" vitamins, and there were some minerals in them. I decided to keep this patient going for a little while to see if indeed this could have been due to a vitamin deficiency. This proved to be the case. Simply, with these vitamins, she was a new woman, and, even after a long time, continued to bloom, confirming again the deficiencies, either in vitamins, minerals or trace elements, can be the cause of nervous disorders, even to the extent of causing quite deep depression. At the moment, the national press writes about the worry of some groups of doctors and psychiatrists in the United States. They are concerned about children who become too diet-conscious and, when they cut out certain foods which we regard as good foods, their health suffers to the extent that brain damage can result. Parents seem to have such an influence on children that diet plays a most important part in their minds, thus causing a deficiency of certain elements. This creates great problems. Besides anorexia nervosa, young people can become not only paranoid, but almost obsessive about their food pattern. One should be very careful with this.

We do know, in whatever country of the world we live, that the soil from which we eat is all different and, in this part of the world, I sometimes feel very worried about the lack of certain minerals. If food is grown organically one should get all the minerals and vitamins that one needs, but the soil in many parts of the world is so dead because of chemical interference, that deficiencies can be expected. Organically grown food has undoubtedly much more to offer than all the artificially grown products. Pesticides have a damaging effect as well as artificial manuring. In our own organic nursery we know that the taste and the smell of our products is superior. More important, from the several tests we have been doing, we know that the minerals and trace elements are of much higher value than those of products which are delivered from non-organic growing. It is quite surprising to see that a simple mineral like zinc, which is deficient in our Scottish soil, can be the cause of so many ailments. We do know, with anorexia nervosa, and even with some physical illnesses, that zinc is sometimes a great help. In a test we did with watercress, this proved to be so rich in minerals and trace elements that we always advise it to be used as a daily supplement.

Sometimes there are cases with which we deal, diagnosed as being anorexia nervosa, or results of food deficiencies, which, with some simple minerals, can be greatly helped. To mind comes a promising young ballet dancer. When I saw her before she went abroad, she was a most attractive girl, and every letter I received from her said that she felt fine, until suddenly I stopped hearing from her. Then, unexpectedly, she came back home and her parents were in a great state of alarm. In the part of the world in which she had been, she became suddenly quite lonely, started to eat less, and her weight dropped so much that she looked like a skeleton when she came back. I hardly recognised her when her parents brought her to me. She was obviously diagnosed as being anorexic, but, talking to her, and getting a bit more information from her, I found she did not have all the symptoms of Anorexia Nervosa. What she did have was a deficiency of vitamins, minerals and trace elements. When I started her treatment I used zinc and vitamins as a basic strengthening programme. Soon she started to respond and her health improved greatly. On her last visit I was very happy to see her slowly returning back to her normal self. Her old energy and wonderful sense of humour was gradually returning.

This brings to mind another young person I saw in one of my clinics down south. She was diagnosed as having a mental illness which caused great physical aggressiveness, making her almost impossible to live with. Actually she did suffer from an illness called Pellagra. It seemed that this particular lady had gone on a diet, using some pep pills to curb her appetite, and succeeded in losing a tremendous lot of weight. She felt so clear in her mind that she thought it was doing her a lot of good. Basically, she was suffering from malnutrition. Her brain and nerve cells had suffered. Luckily she reacted very well when I started her on a course of Vitamin B6 and Vitamin C, with a very well balanced diet. I might point out, that with these patients where there has been a clear deficiency, I always introduce a balanced diet, rich in soya. Soya is always beneficial to such people. We also find with soya, that when used on ageing people, a dietary supplement is needed — potassium, B Vitamins, sometimes chromium, selenium and others. Senior citizens often have difficulty in digesting their food. Sometimes this is the result of not buying nutritionally adequate meals, and eating foods which are deficient because of too long storage. In these cases one has to add a supplement, especially when there is a history of sleeplessness and nerves. Many older people show a lack of Vitamin C, and, when concentration becomes difficult, psychiatrists often advise the use of Vitamin B3, Vitamin B6, Vitamin E, Vitamin B12 and Vitamin C in combination. These sometimes give surprising results. The ageing brain and nervous system need more proteins, vitamins and minerals, and in larger amounts than younger people, and it is, without a doubt, when attention is given to this, that we keep our older people mentally fit and happy. Shortage of good protein, and I have seen this in the Far East, can have some nasty repercussions. One does not need too much protein, as, in our Western countries, this is very often grossly overdone, but we do know that these proteins which we need should be of good quality. It is a great worry that sometimes in bigger institutes too much tinned food is used, and there are deficiencies in iron, calcium, and other minerals, as well as trace elements. This, due to processing, can be the cause of some nasty symptoms and, because of that, vitamins and food supplements are necessary. This is a pity, because, if our food were taken as natural as possible and grown in the appropriate soil, there would be no need for all this. The health food shops and vitamin factories could close their businesses, but, unfortunately, because of deficiencies in our food, we need to supplement with extra factory-made products.

In today's establishment we have to well understand that vitamins, tissue salts, trace elements, minerals, are needed for good health, and if deficiencies do occur on this point, one has to work out a programme for correcting that. There are some very serious physical and mental illnesses which cause irreparable damage because not enough attention was paid to them. It is quite true that certain deficiencies are very difficult to diagnose and one can be completely baffled. Prevention, however, is better than cure, and it is well to advise that one should use food, vegetables and products which are rich in calcium and iodine as an antidote. Again, a case comes to mind of a middle-aged patient who was difficult to diagnose in this particular field, and, because she was slightly overweight, I found that she was eating most of the wrong foods. I put her on some vitamins and quite a high dosage of Kelpasan, a kelp product and some tissue salts. The response was quite surprising, she felt so much better because her thyroid had been attacked by the way she lived and by the deficiencies which had occurred. This had made her very nervous, causing upset sleepless nights. She ate the wrong things, which, of course, very often happens. In this respect one can see again that preventive measures should be taken when these little alarm bells in the body tell us that there is something wrong.

Many schizophrenic patients we see go for the wrong kinds of foods, and with the help of large doses of Vitamin B3 and Vitamin C, these wrong-eating habits, which mostly cause deficiencies, can be helped sometimes above expectation. The diet for the schizophrenic, which is rich in Vitamins B and C, gives an improvement in these patients, and we find this with the alcoholic patient as well. Deficiencies sometimes cause a slow child to be thought of as a day-dreamer. Improvement is usually seen when combinations of Vitamin B6, Vitamin C and Vitamin E are administered. After several tests were done, the results, within a few weeks, were quite obvious. It is essential, therefore, that vitamins, minerals, trace elements and enzymes, which are missing in food or destroyed by cooking, processing, etc., should be watched carefully when treating patients with nerve-related problems. Again to my mind comes a male patient who had been under tremendous stress, worrying both financially and domestically. He gradually lost nearly all his hair and became almost bald. He consulted me and pleaded for help. When tests were done his liver was found to be affected. I gave him some homoeopathic remedies in addition to Vitamin PP factor. After much patience and persevering his hair eventually grew in again.

I have already described several cases where there is a definite link between food deficiencies, vitamin deficiencies and mineral deficiencies, in the spectrum of mental or nervous disorders. Too often we find that these deficiencies are the last thing we suspect in treating patients and, quite unfairly, patients are sometimes branded as neurotics. They respond well to treatment. Hyperactive nervous children are greatly helped by a drastic change of diet. Cut out food additives and too much sugar.

All these problems show again that the right communication between doctor, practitioner, and patient should be established. In the next chapter on COMMUNICATION I do hope that this will also help to solve the problems of these so lightly looked at disorders of today's society.

15

Communication

LONELINESS, which is one of the principal causes of depression, is often rooted in a failure to communicate.

I was forcefully reminded of this early one morning in a London underground station. It wasn't the cheeriest of places to be at 6 am on a cold winter's day. I saw a few drunks, a man who was an obvious drug addict and several drop-outs lying along the station platform. I felt lonely, as one can be, in the heart of a great city. But my spirits were raised when I noticed a British Telecom advert in my own language stressing how easy it was to communicate with the folks back home in Holland. All I had to do was lift a telephone. I was still in touch. Even the thought brightened my outlook in contrast to the obvious deep misery of the drunks, addicts and others, who had opted out of communication with their fellow human beings.

What had gone wrong in their lives? What had prompted them to turn their back on society? I thought of these questions and of what is surely one of the big contradictions in human society towards the end of the twentieth century.

On the one hand, science and technology have brought the peoples of the world closer by providing the means of communication over thousands of miles of land and sea. On the other hand, millions of people suffer from aches and pains, shocks and depression, high and low moods and breakdowns, often because of a failure to make contact with their immediate neighbours.

It can be spiritually uplifting to escape occasionally from "The Madding Crowd", from the hurly-burly and the mounting pressures of modern society, to indulge in what has been described in poetic language as "mingling with the universe" on a glorious summer's day. The trouble starts when the need to escape becomes an obsession. A person's mind, in such circumstances, is constantly turned inwards and the door is firmly locked against any unwanted intruders.

Man is basically a social animal. Without co-operating in distant primitive times he would never have survived against the fiercer, stronger animals of the jungle. Today, perhaps more than ever, there is a need for peoples and nations to pull together. There is a tendency to think of communication as a nation-to-nation bringing together of peoples by means of pictures beamed via satellites in outer space and shown on television screens.

Real communication, however, is much more basic and has its origins in the day-to-day relationships of people in their homes, in buses and trains, and in their places of work. In this context the question of language, the capacity to use words, is of paramount importance. Words can do good but they can also do harm. A doctor's spoken reassurance at a patient's bedside is often the best form of "medicine", but words can also be instruments of evil, as Doctor Goebbels found when he was weaving them into propaganda for spreading the hideous doctrines of Nazism.

In normal human relationships words aren't always needed. Very often a smile or a wink is all that is necessary to establish a friendly understanding between two people, whereas a frown or a grimace can convey the opposite. Even body movements can speak volumes about a person's attitude without the need to speak. A number of years ago sticking up your thumb was a very meaningful gesture. A simple nod of the head can be a sign of approval or agreement. And wasn't it the famous Churchillian Victory sign which did so much to boost the morale of the British during the Second World War? After all, everyone's very first attempt to communicate is made without words. The cry of a baby is usually an attempt to attract the attention of the mother. Even in the first two months, when it cannot smile, it can display the early signs of an individual personality in appealing looks and facial expressions.

The first few months can be a vital period in a person's life. More often than not a wonderful rapport is established between mother and child. A mother's love is an essential ingredient in giving a baby happiness and security and determining whether or not it grows up into a well-balanced man or woman.

In many cases, however, children are born into homes where there is no love, where because of poverty there are constant rows between parents. The "wee souls" are crying out with every instinct to be loved and cherished and when they are shown no affection the seeds are sown for problems in later life — people become withdrawn, unhappy and unable to communicate with others. This is why psychiatrists, in looking for reasons for ailments of the mind, are often so deeply concerned with establishing where communication has gone wrong between a mother and her child.

Today we live in a world where communication is more necessary than ever before. In the "I am" diagram we see that the soul, which is the fountainhead of all that is spiritual in our lives, influences and colours our disposition and consequently our method of communication. Communication isn't always expressed in words spoken or written, but in that undefineable aspect of human relations called understanding. Two people who live with each other know by intuition if or not they are in harmony or on the same wavelength and working together as a two-way process. Depending on the need, of course, the couple will come and go, allowing each other to give and take as they need to.

Good communication, resulting in happy human relationships, can be, as I have already suggested, a wonderful therapy in helping to cure psychosomatic illnesses. It can build up a smoothly-functioning rapport between mind and body, making for happiness and health. Yet, disturbingly, I don't think there has ever been such a lack of communication as there is in present-day society.

I often recall the days in Holland when the Second World War was finished. We had been occupied by the Nazis. A mood of relief enveloped the entire country. Everyone was united in sharing one desire — to have one religion, one political party, and never ever to go through the traumas of war again. The feeling was one of escaping from a nightmare into a new world of freedom and high hopes. Looking back at my country today, in defiance of all that was so promising in the immediate aftermath of war, we have the world's highest number of political parties, as well as possibly the highest number of religious denominations.

What real prospects are there for world peace if even in a domestic situation there is a breakdown in communication, resulting in a record number of marriages ending in divorce? Where has communication gone wrong? This is a question I have often asked myself. The reasons are numerous. One thing is certain — where there is negative thinking, leading to emotional disturbance, where a husband and wife are out of harmony with each other and the wedding-day dreams of bliss are replaced by fear or resentment, the Life Force is seriously inhibited in its efforts to keep the body functioning in top gear.

Even much earlier in life, among children at school, education often suffers because of a lack of communication between teacher and pupil. Sometimes the various stages of physical and mental development are underestimated by the teacher and some children, far from ever realising their full potential, are forced to leave school classified as "failures" — a stigma on their young, impressionable minds from which they seldom recover.

One of the big problems I have found in treating people suffering from severe depression is the tremendous difficulty they experience in trying to communicate. Yet it would be much easier to help them, and indeed for them to help themselves, if they could influence their soul and Life Force with positive thoughts and hopes of recovery. All of which, as far as the person suffering from depression is concerned, is easier said than done! This is actually the core of the problem and can often lie deeply buried in the dark recesses of the patient's subconscious mind.

I remember an old professor once telling me that an excellent remedy for a feeling of despair or depression was for a person to return to the place of his or her birth — to go back, in a sense, to the beginning. At one point in my life, soon after I came to live in

Scotland, I was experiencing a depression about certain things and decided to try out the professor's advice. I booked a seat on a plane to Holland and went straight to the place where I had come into the world. I was walking across a bridge which connected the small railway with the town, when I "bumped into" a person I hadn't seen for at least twenty years. Much to my surprise he said, "Hello, Jan", and kept on walking, treating me as if I had never been away! These two friendly words, spoken with some warmth, acted as an instant tonic and dispersed the clouds of depression, completely vindicating the claims of the old professor. His advice I have since passed on to my patients who found it worked for them too. Is this, I wonder, why so many people in their later years develop a nostalgia for the place in which they were born?

There are so many ways, apart from speaking, in which a person can communicate. I was present at a graduation ceremony recently and the Vice-President of the Red Cross said a few words which I felt were so true. She told the medical graduates that hands were a wonderful way of communicating between doctor and patient. Even by a simple touch, she said, feelings could be expressed which could restore broken communications.

Sometimes communication with a patient looks impossible. I remember one particular patient who consulted me. He was suffering from deep depression. When I started to speak to him there was minimal response. I got the feeling I often have when I dial a telephone number and find myself speaking to an answering machine. My patient appeared to be just as cold and impersonal, staring ahead with dull, listless eyes as if nothing in life any longer interested him. Before he had entered my consulting room, I noticed him touching our staircase which is made from the finest oak wood. I asked him what he thought of the wood, with little hope of response. I was surprised, therefore, when I suddenly realised I had got through to him. His eyes lit up and he looked straight into my eyes where he found understanding. His form of communication wasn't in speech but in touch, and the excellent woodwork had apparently brought back to life an earlier sense of pride in craftmanship. This was the key to opening him up — a "golden" key which, after several sessions, helped me to bring a new brightness back into his life. One needs to communicate to learn the ability to be genuinely interested in some area of life.

Mental attitude can be a vital factor in influencing success or failure. This was brought home to me recently at a lecture by a famous specialist in the field of communication. He asked two violinists present at this lecture to play a tune. The first player, after tuning up her instrument, stopped and asked the audience if they thought her playing would be good or bad. They all said they thought it would be good, not out of sympathy or good manners, but because of the way she was holding her violin and bow and by the confident expression on her face. The second player was possibly more accomplished but she had a different mental attitude and her playing, though good, didn't have quite the same flow as that of the other girl. She was asked if she had any feeling for, or communication with, her instrument which was a work of art, apart from the music it provided. Surprisingly, she replied: "Not particularly. To me, it's just a bit of wood."

She was then asked to call her violin Peter which was her boyfriend's name, and play again. This time there was a slight improvement in her playing but the specialist remarked that it wasn't as good as it ought to be. At this the girl broke down in tears and was asked to go into the neighbouring room, to sort herself out, and then to come back. I was surprised to see that she did come back and when she played it was much better. Obviously she was a good violinist, but she had a problem related to her mental attitude. This problem came to light when she was asked to call her violin by her mother's name. She broke down in tears again. Apparently as a child she had been forced by her mother to play the violin and to practise for long hours while her friends were indulging in more pleasurable things. Ever since, one part of her mind had been revelling in her musical ability while the other part was still rebelling at the memory of parental discipline.

This kind of inner conflict in the mind is so often the cause of such problems as inferiority complex and stage fright — problems which, as I mentioned earlier, are often related to a breakdown between mother and child.

It was also interesting to note that that first violin player had been through some nasty experiences and at the time had not wanted to communicate with anyone. One day she picked up her violin, had a feeling of communication with it, and her playing improved no end.

Such problems where there is a breakdown in communication often need only be acknowledged by the patient in order to start disintegrating. One day in the parking place at my clinic, I noticed a perfect example of intelligent communication between dogs. A little poodle came out of a car and, to my horror, our two big hounds stormed at great speed towards it, growling fiercely. I held my breath, fearing that the little dog would be torn to pieces. Suddenly the poodle, as if guided by instinct, just rolled over on its back saying, in effect, to the two monsters: "Do with me what you like!" The violent intentions of the huge animals were punctured by non-violent resistance — a form of communication which left them bewildered as they backed off, their growling now distinctly muted and their tails firmly placed between their legs!

Another form of communication is the love relationship which a man can have with his car. This kind of relationship involves great care, attention, and communication, and means fewer breakdowns. It brings a story concerning Henry Ford to my mind. The famous American car maker was driving in his dinner suit to a social function, when he noticed a car broken down on the road and the driver looking on with obvious helplessness. Henry Ford ordered his chauffeur to stop, went over to the car and asked what the trouble was. The young man in charge of the vehicle looked disdainfully at the well-dressed distinguished gentleman and muttered: "You wouldn't know what to do". He went on staring at the car. The man in evening dress did know what to do, and when the boy finally agreed to let him have a go, he got the engine running smoothly again by no more than a simple adjustment. "How in the world did you do it so quickly?" asked the young man with surprise and relief. "Because I happen to have built this type of car," Ford replied.

Certainly Henry Ford knew how to communicate. As one of the first makers of cars, he also learned how to communicate with people.

Finally, one of the most impressive lessons on the vital role of communications I ever came across in my practice concerned a charming couple whose marriage looked as if it was heading for the rocks. The wife came to me first and when she pleaded with me to save her marriage, I asked if I could see her husband, in the belief that there are always two sides to a story of damaged relationships. Luckily he came to see me and was most co-opera-tive. One morning, when he had obviously made up his mind to leave her, I asked him to do a final thing for me. I asked him to delay any decision until the evening and to compile during the day a list of his wife's positive and negative points. His wife had been asked to do the same and I agreed with him that if her negative points were much higher than the positive ones, he could make his decision to leave her.

Unfortunately, in the afternoon when he came to deliver his list, the negative points were indeed a lot higher. I then made a telephone call to his wife to ask if her list was ready. In tears she said she couldn't do it. She had written a letter and put it on his pillow. It said: "I accepted you as you were when we were married with all your negatives and all your positives, and I accept you now, just as you are."

This candid approach was enough to repair the broken communications between them and enough to make them feel very much happier. It was a timely reminder of the truth that even with the best of couples, even in the most blissful of marriage relationships, there are negative and positive aspects. This reminds me of the words of St Paul who shows us in the thirteenth Corinthians, verse two, an even more excellent way to communicate: "If I have the gift of prophecy, and understand all mysteries and all knowledge, and if I have faith that can remove mountains, but have not LOVE, I am nothing."

Bibliography and Literature

Toussaint, J D — *Ziekte als Lot En Kans* (First Edition 1972), Ankh-Hermes, Deventer, Holland

Horne, Ross — *The Health Revolution* (First Edition 1980), Ross Horne, Avalon Beach, NSW, Australia

Ferguson, Marilyn — *The Aquarian Conspiracy* (First Edition 1981), Routledge and Kegan Paul Ltd., London

Ferguson, Marilyn — *The Merck Manual* (Eighth Edition), Merck and Co. Inc., Rahway NJ, USA

Durckheim von Karlfried Graf — *"HARA": The Vital Centre of Man* (Mandala Edition 1977), George Allan & Unwin Ltd., London

Vogel, A — *The Nature Doctor* (Eighth Edition 1977), Verlag A Vogel Teufen/AR/Switzerland

Schwab, Gunther — *Bij de Duivel te Gast* (First Edition), De Driehoek, Amsterdam

Schaldach, Herbert — *Grundlagen Der Medizin Für Heilberufe* (First Edition 1955), Veb Verlag Volk Und Gesundheit, Berlin, Germany

Buchinger, Otto — *Das Heilfasten* (Eighth Edition), Hippokrates-Verlag Marquardt and Cie, Stuttgart, Germany

BY APPOINTMENT ONLY

Benaïche, Robert — *Le Friedmann Dans La Therapeutique De La Tuberculose*, André Martel, Paris, France

Dextreit, Raymond — *Les Maladies De La Femme*, Editions De La Revue *Vivre en Harmonie*, Paris, France

Robert, Herbert, A — *The Principles and Art of Cure by Homoeopathy*, Hom. Pub. Comp., London

Wheeler, F J, M.R.C.S., L.R.C.P. — *The Bach Remedies Repertory*, The Daniel Co. Ltd., London

Index

BY APPOINTMENT ONLY